the
re.
view

how
&
what
for

Tulane University
Academic Year 2020-2021

Editor
Andrea Bardon de Tena

Publication Assistants
Gabe Darley, Chelsea Kilgore, Giuliana Vaccarino Gearty

Copy Editing
Alexia Narun

Publisher
ACTAR

HEADER KEY

s>	**i>**	**UG**	**GR**	**[C]**
student	instructor	undergraduate	graduate in blue	coordinator

CONTENTS

Iñaki Alday

Dean, Richard Koch Chair in Architecture

Introduction to the ReView

This edition of The ReView communicates the pedagogical project and some of the lines of research of the Tulane School of Architecture (TuSA) through the work, mostly visual, of its students and professors. As in any educational project, the essential questions are "what for?" and "how?"

Tulane is recognized as one of the great American schools of architecture — despite its small size — with a history of 130 years educating excellent professionals. Professional quality continues to be a nonnegotiable objective. Our original program — the 5-year professional degree in architecture — remains the trunk of a tree that has grown with powerful branches: masters and other undergraduate programs. In 1998, the school began to offer an essential program, preservation, for one of the cities of greatest historical value in the country: New Orleans. And in 2011, we added sustainable real estate development. Today, all of these programs — architecture, preservation, real estate — are growing and being completed by design and — shortly — environmental engineering and landscape architecture. Covering the full spectrum of the built environment not only allows us to contribute great professionals to all these fields, but also to address the next level of our goals: to rethink the way we are building the planet.

It is true that one of the main attributes of a university is its eagerness to produce knowledge for the shake of it, without the need for a practical application: "A university should house and honor anarchic provocation and the passion for uselessness" [1]. But it is also true that we are in an unprecedented environmental crisis that demands the urgent production of applicable knowledge. Tulane has been characterized, since its birth in 1834 as a medical college to combat yellow fever, for combining its two academic souls: free intellectual exploration and the immediate impact on the serious crises of the moment.

New Orleans is an exceptional place to educate oneself and to research about the built environment. An international metropolis since its foundation — the main port of the Gulf, French, Spanish and American, center of cultural and merchandise exchange — epitomizes the social and ecological challenges of a large part of the cities and territories of the planet. Although many of them are in similar geographical situations, New Orleans is located in one of the most paradigmatic places: the mouth of one of the largest rivers and one of the most important and threatened deltas: the Mississippi. As a port and international city since its birth, New Orleans is one of the most intense and complex cultural crossroads on the planet, a cradle of music and arts, gastronomy, languages, races and, of course, architecture. TuSA leverages its status as an extraordinary universal model by working in New Orleans and Louisiana in parallel to other regions of the world — Southeast Asia, Central Africa, Europe, and Latin America.

The chapter "How?" exposes the pedagogical methodologies of programs of exceptional quality. Real Estate Development is housed in the school of architecture at Tulane, not in business, and includes studio: the physical design of development operations. In New Orleans, preservation has the richest physical laboratory one can imagine, from Native American settlements to the modern mid-century, through all of the architectural history that makes this city

1. Steiner, George, 2013, Universitas, Nexus Instituut

5

the richest cultural amalgam in North America. Design is not so much a professional specialty as it is a basic education for efficiency in a world where everything, from places to objects and experiences, is designed. The construction of competences in architecture combines education with creativity, the deep knowledge of the history that makes architecture a cultural activity, the development of visual and spatial thinking, and the preparation for the lifelong learning of rapidly evolving technologies, both digital and material. They all share an emphasis on complexity and the ability to holistically understand problems and collaborate within and across disciplines.

The chapter "What for?" exposes some of the themes explored at TuSA. Climate change and its impact on communities, from the transformation of land uses and value to the adaptation of architecture and public spaces, is a central theme common to all programs. Architecture, preservation, real estate development, landscape architecture, and design are critical fields for addressing the greatest threat to humanity. And the university is the place where those who are going to fight against climate change and its consequences are educated, as well as the place where research takes place and knowledge is produced for the same purpose. Our work in New Orleans, Addis Ababa, New Delhi, Ecuador, and other places in America and the world addresses all scales — from planning to material research in permeable grounds, through neighborhoods, infrastructures, architectural typologies, heritage recovery, economic and social dynamics, and built investigations for the use of our community partners.

The conceptual link that connects the "How?" and the "What for?" is the idea of innovation. Of course, research projects try to bring new knowledge to the disciplinary field. On the other hand, some of the pedagogical proposals are in themselves innovative: the sequence of theory and history, the abandonment of the "survey" practice, or the commitment of "research studios" to bring a project to the classroom for three years. However, the main underlying effort is to educate innovators. Some of the "core studios" are firmly committed to challenging basic skills with ambitious questions with no obvious answer, such as explorations in intentional communities and urbanism in the study of collective housing. The same goes for the thesis requirement for undergraduates, which asks each student to consider for a year how to contribute — modestly, of course — to architectural knowledge.

Effective innovation is reinforced by two fundamental supports: understanding real needs through direct work with communities — Small Center for Collaborative Design — and the testing and evaluation of solutions, designed and built or examined by organizations and governments. The school is not locked in an ivory tower, but strongly — sometimes starkly — exposed to an outside world as threatening as it is exciting.

Neither in the East nor West, TuSA is the school of the third American coast. Our location, history, and exposure to the front line of social and environmental challenges force us to be independent. In this position we can define, without waiting or following anyone, the role and capabilities of architects, designers, urban planners, real estate developers, and preservationists who are going to transform the way we are inhabiting this planet.

Jesse M. Keenan

Favrot II Professor of Real Estate

From an Architecture School to a School of the Built Environment

The Tulane School of Architecture is in the midst of a transformation from an architecture school to a school of the built environment. In terms of the compositional identity of this school, this transformation is a reflection of the diversity of faculty within the school including social scientists, geographers, graphic designers, preservationists, historians, lawyers, economists, civil engineers, landscape architects, urban planners, and real estate developers. These faculty represent new perspectives about the form and process of the built environment. These ideas are drawn from novel areas of academic inquiry, as well as from students, communities, practitioners, and stakeholders — who see the design and management of the built environment as a penultimate exercise on the frontier of addressing some of the world's most pressing challenges and opportunities.

On this frontier, professional and economic allegiances that have reinforced structural inequalities and environmental degradations challenge the conventions of practice and of the utility within the strictures of professional qualification and development. Yet, the light is not dimming for architecture, rather it is casting its own pedagogical reflection on these allied programs of the built environment. Research studios at the school are pushing the limits of cross-scalar representation and thematic exploration unknown to prior generations of architects. While mastery is paramount to the refinement of professional excellence, so too is the expanded horizons from which design methods are applied across the disciplines. Here, design is at the heart of the problem-solution nexus that stimulates our global anxieties for the fragility of the built environment.

Some people may be rightly nostalgic for the primacy of architecture. There is a cultural dimension to architectural education that created social and intellectual bonds that have endured for generations. The legacy position of architectural disciplinarity is not diluted by the multiple disciplines of the built environment. To the contrary, architecture has long relied on and has contributed to the foundation of everything from estate management (later real estate development) to landscape architecture, and from construction management to urban design. The faculty of early American architecture schools were populated by a broad array of technicians, trades, and applied scientists. It was not uncommon at the turn of the 20th century to see economists and engineers serving on design juries at America's leading architecture schools. The design and construction of buildings and cities was viewed as multidisciplinary — not transdisciplinary. It was not until the mid-20th century that academic disciplinary specialization, professional licensure, and risk management forced architects, urban designers, civil engineers, and planners to go their separate ways. A final hold-out of this long-forgotten era is bridge design, which still persists in many architecture schools.

Today, there is an intellectual shift across America's architecture and design schools. Students and faculty are exhausted by the endless modern, postmodern, and post-postmodern tropes that were once profound critiques of material solutions to problems that are now superseded by the rapidity of global change. Performance, impact, exposure, inclusion and experience — which also reject the metaphysics of phenomenology — drive a new form of empirical accountability in architecture and architectural education. There is a revolution in building and material science that is now integral to both conceptual design and material specification across an expanded lifecycle of the building. Building users are not frictionless automatons in a computation fluid dynamic model or interpreters of critical regionalism. Rather, they are living and breathing people with lived experiences that may extend across generations in a single building. They are also constructors, managers, and designers in their own right who co-design the built environment long after construction contracts have been closed out. Community planners are learning real estate finance, and developers are dedicating their studies to historic preservation. The boundaries of professional qualifications are blurred now more than ever in both practice and academia. Whether this is a form of critical realism that has supplanted a prior regime of positivism or poststructuralism is for the historians to sort out.[1] In the face of rapid technological, economic, and social change, what we do know is that all of the disciplines of the built environment are recognizing that interdisciplinary learning and practice provides safety in numbers.

Tulane has led the way in building a foundation for interdisciplinary studies in the built environment. The school's design-build, social innovation, community design, and sustainable real estate programs were introduced years ahead of any other American school. These programs laid the foundation for an array of majors and programs that have opened the door for a broader cohort of students with a greater diversity of interests and skills. There are now more dual majors across the programs of the school than at any time before. As the school begins to inhale new people and ideas, it also must exhale the vestiges of isolation that comes along with narrow accreditation requirements and peer-to-peer benchmarking.

1. Næss, P. (2015). Critical realism, urban planning and urban research. European Planning Studies, 23(6), 1228-1244.

It is no coincidence that the blurred lines of personal and cultural identify have spilled over into organizational and institutional realms. In a highly uncertain state (i.e., the world we live in), agility and flexibility are superior attributes to fixity and stationarity. For some of us, this is a moment of liberation tempered only by an obligation for rigor, discipline, and critical reflection. For others, this is the beginning of the end of the sacred order. The thing about transformations and revolutions is that valuable knowledge can forever be lost. Closer to home, the challenge is to preserve the sacred disciplinary-specific canonical knowledge without being beholden to its historical uses and misuses. This means disciplining our contemporary impulses for historicization and presentism. Emancipatory ontologies create new knowledge — they do not replace knowledge through social norms.

A shift to a school of the built environment is not a revolution co-aligned with external events. Rather it is part of a long evolution of non-disciplinary practices in design, construction, and management that have endured since the dawn of civilization. In this (pre-)historical context, a school of the built environment is merely a reversion to the unbounded generalist knowledge of the architect. In the future, as we formalize our commitment to a united intellectual pursuit in the name of the built environment, we have the opportunity to find a common humility in our co-existence that is central to our collective survival. As survivalists, we all must be generalists.

"The real problem of humanity is [that] we have Paleolithic emotions, medieval institutions, and god-like technology."

E.O. Wilson

Edson Cabalfin
Associate Dean for Equity, Diversity & Inclusion

Towards Equity, Diversity, and Inclusion at Tulane School of Architecture

What do we mean by equity, diversity, and inclusion (EDI)? And how does equity, diversity, and inclusion intersect with the work of Tulane School of Architecture?

Let us define a couple of terms first. Equity refers to the "state, quality, or ideal of being just, impartial, or fair."[1] This can refer to how the built environment provides a level-playing field for everyone to live and thrive. Diversity means acknowledging the "differences among social groups such as ethnic heritage, class, age, gender, sexuality, ability, religion, and nationality."[2] By this, we can understand how the built environment recognizes and respects the differing lived experiences and backgrounds of people who are living together. And by inclusion, we may mean "the leveraging of difference by integrating diverse perspectives and creating a better outcome for all."[3]   In including a diverse group of people and experiences, we also recognize how different voices can contribute to the creation of the built environment.[4]   Equity, diversity, and inclusion are ideals that are interconnected and overlapping, each mutually reinforcing another.

It is abundantly clear that the built environment is inextricably intertwined with issues of equity, diversity, and

1. "Embracing Equity: 7 Steps to Advance and Embed Race Equity and Inclusion Within Your Organization", (Annie Casey Foundation, 2014).

2. Lee Anne Bell, "Theoretical Foundations for Social Justice Education" in Teaching for Diversity and Social Justice, 3rd Edition, edited by Maurianne Adams, Lee Anne Bell, Diane Goodman, Khyati Joshi, (London: Routledge, 2016), p. 3.

3. Creative Reaction Lab, Equity-Centered Community Design, (St. Louis, MO: Creative Reaction Lab, 2018).

4. Kathryn Anthony, Designing for Diversity: Gender, Race, and Ethnicity in the Architectural Profession, (Urbana-Champaign, IL: University of Illinois Press, 2001).

Fig. 1 (Right)
Professor Edson Cabalfin, hosting the 2022 Data X Community X Design workshop.

inclusion. In fact, architecture and our man-made environment always had a part in how people from certain segments of the population have been historically excluded, oppressed, and marginalized. Examples, such as redlining neighborhoods, creating ghettoes, spatial segregation, among others have all pointed out to how oppression works by design.[5] If some of these systemic ways of oppression were created with malice in the first place, then there is also the opportunity to design for liberation and empowerment.

At the Tulane School of Architecture, equity, diversity, and inclusion are at the core of its mission as an educational institution. We cannot separate our role in nurturing the next generation of our practitioners of the built environment from ensuring that what we teach, research, and practice advocates for a more just, diverse, equitable, and inclusive future. As such, substantial work has been ac-

5. Richard Rothstein, The Color of Law: A Forgotten History of How Our Government Segregated America, (New York: Liveright, 2018); Carl H. Nightingale, Segregation: A Global History of Divided Cities, (Chicago and London: University of Chicago Press, 2012); Kathryn Anthony, Defined by Design: The Surprising Power of Hidden Gender, Age, and Body Bias in Everyday Products and Places, (New York: Prometheus Books, 2017; Amin Ghazani, There Goes the Gayborhood, Princeton, NJ and Oxford: Princeton University Press, 2014); Keenga-Yamahtta Taylor, Race for Profit: How Banks and the Real Estate Industry Undermined Black Homeownership, (Durham, NC: University of North Carolina Press, 2019).

June 2020
Creation of the Task Force for Racial Equity, Diversity, and Inclusion that looked at the current state of EDI in the school.

January 2021
REDI Task Force submitted final report to the TuSA Faculty, which led to the appointment of Edson Cabalfin as the inaugural Associate Dean for EDI.

March 2021
Launch and admission of three new Boudreaux Scholarships for historically underrepresented and underserved graduate students; Creation of a new EDI Subcommittee of the Dean's Alumni Council; creation of a new EDI award for a graduating TuSA student.

October 2021
REI Groundwater and VISIONS EDI and anti-racism training for faculty were held.

February 2021
Creation of a new EDI page on TuSA website to communicate EDI issues and content. A new EDI standing committee was created composed of faculty, staff, and students. Launch of new Tulane Architecture Fellows as part of the Dean's Equity and Inclusion Initiative, a national consortium of architecture schools in the US working together towards diversifying faculty.

complished in our equity, diversity, and inclusion work in the school in the last two years. Some of the highlights are as shown on the timeline above.

While much has been achieved in these past couple of years, we also acknowledge that there is still a great deal of work that lies ahead of us. Since systems of oppression have been in place for centuries, we cannot expect that we will simply dismantle and redesign them overnight. This task is also not the work of only one person nor of one organization, but is part of a larger network of collaboration that reaches across the personal, interpersonal, institutional, and cultural levels. Within Tulane, the School of Architecture needs to collaborate with other units across campus and the city to truly create an equitable, diverse, and inclusive institution.

In the next couple of years, especially as we set and implement our "Strategy for Tomorrow" 5-year EDI strate-

November 2021
TuSA "Strategy for Tomorrow" Focus Group Discussions, (Part 1) with students, faculty, staff, and alumni as part of the creation of a 5-year EDI Strategic Plan for the university and units.

March 2022
Launch of the new Angela O'Byrne Alumni Award to be given to a TuSA alumni who has demonstrated outstanding community involvement through architecture.

May 2021
Hiring of two Tulane Architecture Fellows; Release of the TuSA Climate Survey that investigated the state of EDI in the school.

February 2022
TuSA "Strategy for Tomorrow" Focus Group Discussions (Part 2) with students, faculty, staff, and alumni to get feedback on the draft of the EDI strategic plan; Creation of a new TuSA Black, Indigenous, and Person of Color (BIPOC) student affinity group.

May 2022
Submission of the final TuSA Strategy for Tomorrow plan to be implemented beginning July 2022.

gic plan, there are still significant and urgent issues that must be addressed. Some of the questions we are asking include: How do we make education on architecture and the built environment accessible to a wider student body? How do we diversify our faculty, staff, and students in the school? How do we support the needs of BIPOC students in the school? How might we redesign our curriculum to include a diverse set of voices and experiences? How do we create a climate that is welcoming and accepting of everyone? How do we create mutually enhancing relationships between the school and community partners across the city?

We all need to participate in making the Tulane School of Architecture a more equitable, diverse, and inclusive institution. We can all work together to ensure that the future generation of leaders, practitioners, and professionals of the built environment contribute to and make a more just, equitable, inclusive, and sustainable future.

how

how

core

Core Studios

Core +

FIRST YEAR DESIGN STUDIO

Desmarais [C]
Crosby | Nasa | Norman | Passarelli

This introductory design studio is the first in a series of core design courses that focus on foundational concepts and methodologies explored through drawing and making. The focus is primarily on immediate and local spatial settings, introducing students to the careful study of the world around them, what can be found there, and what can be imagined to be significant about the shaping of place in an architectural sense.

The goal as each technique is learned is to utilize this expertise as a springboard from which to develop new approaches and unknown solutions. Drawing comprises an architect's primary modes of seeing/thinking/creating and will form the cornerstone for a studio-based process of critical thinking. Students study composition, the nature of something determined by its ingredients or constituents, by observing the way in which a whole is made up of interrelated parts. Building an awareness and understanding of the relationships between parts will propel the design process by generating ideas and defining physical properties with which to work.

The methods for doing so will include workshops that entail material study, free-hand drawing, drafting, constructed perspectives, and 3D modeling. All of these methods will be undertaken to give students a sense of 'how to see,' that is, how to move between both the empirical — what is found through observation and the careful recording of those findings — and the speculative, or the creative formation of what 'might be' as we proceed from recorded information to generative abstraction.

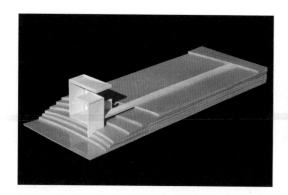
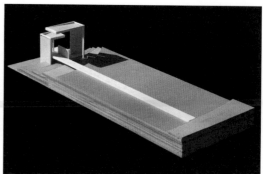

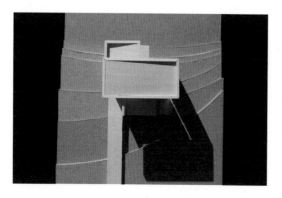

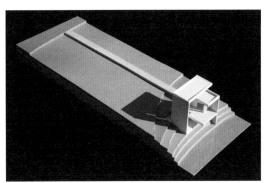

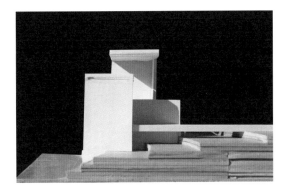
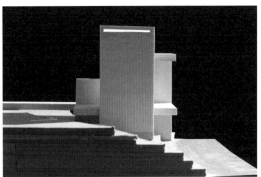

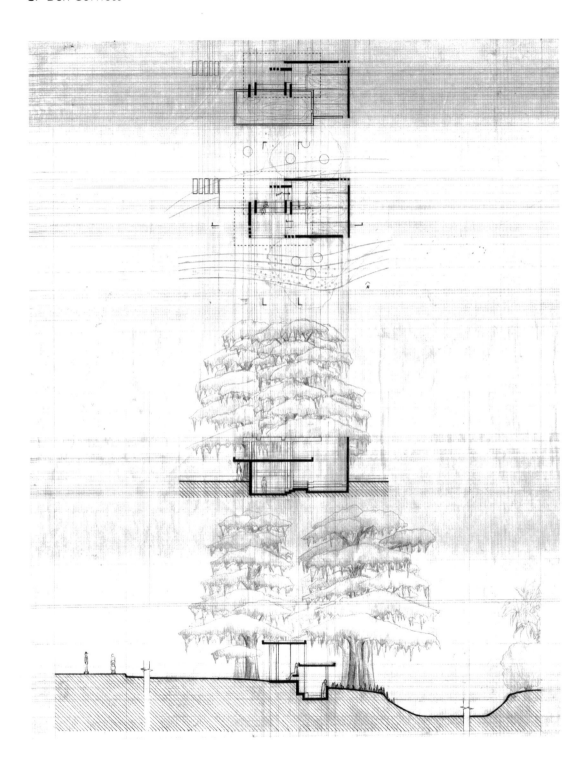

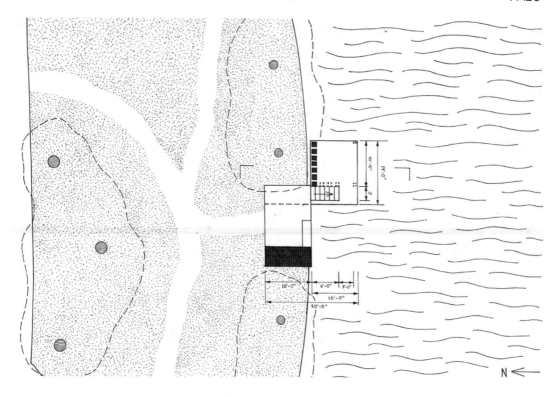

s> Jaime Esquenazi
s> Charlotte Kelley

i> Carrie Norman
i> Marianne Desmarais

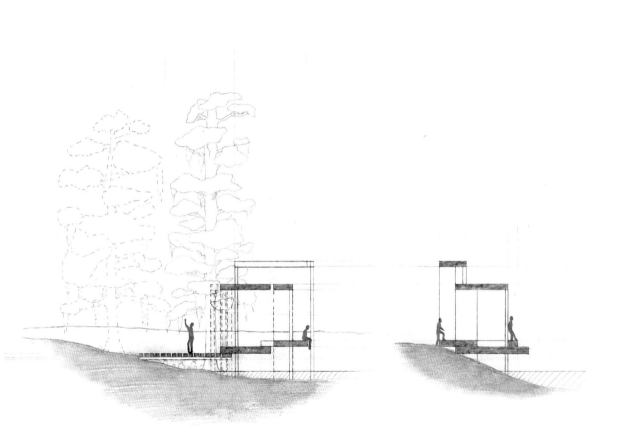

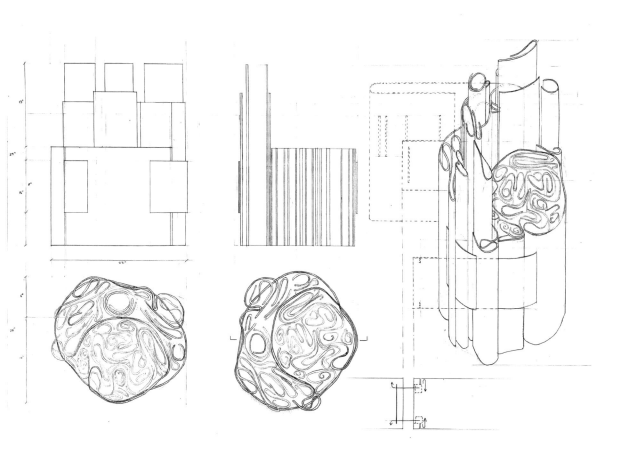

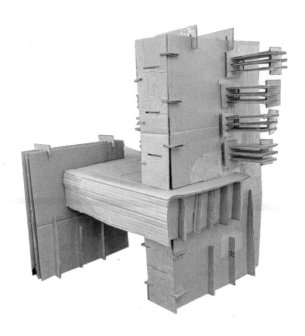

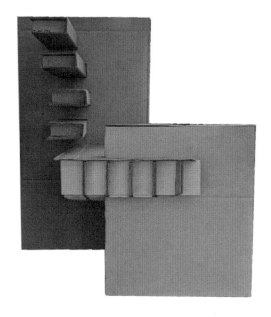

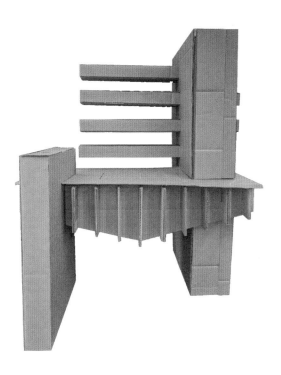

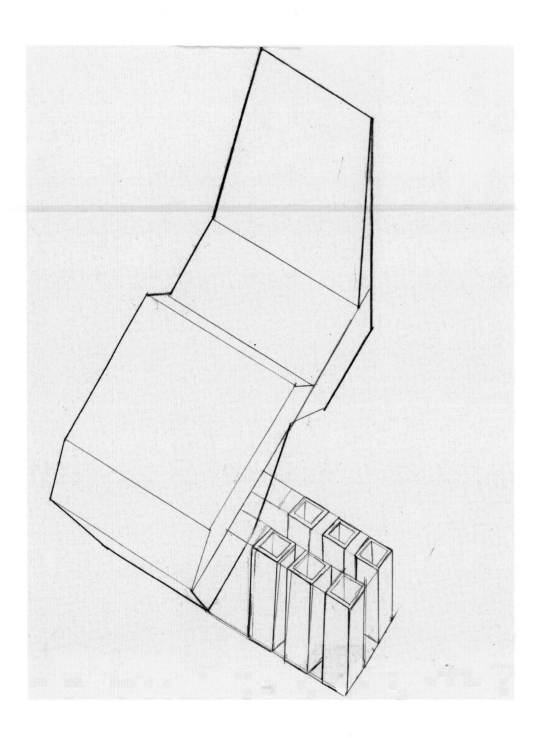

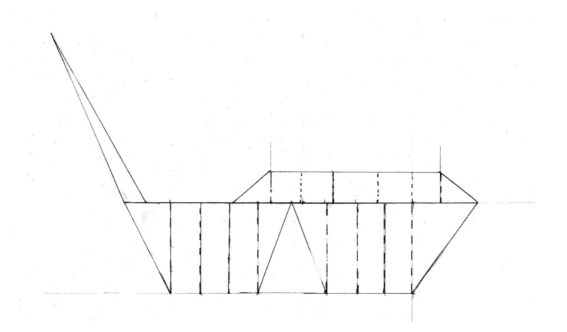

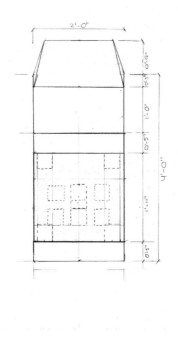

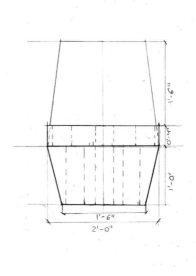

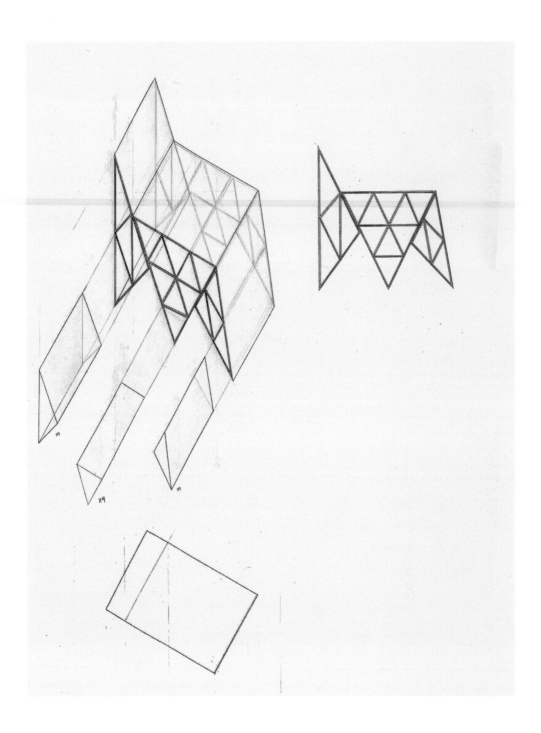

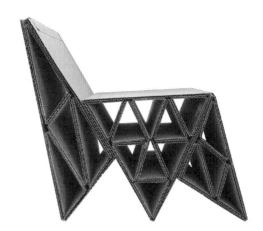

FIRST YEAR CORE STUDIO 2

Modesitt [C]
Crosby | Liles | Redfield | Schwartz

An introduction to the basic fundamental methods and principles of architectural design, students are given an immediate experience of the design process, developing their capacity to conceive, manipulate, and analyze architectural form and space. The studio develops students' capacity for critical thinking through constructive evaluation.

The first year spring architecture/design studio explores the role of form in architecture and design. Form is an expansive term. The definition of form may involve shape, configuration, arrangement, manifestation, type, operative sequence, and performance state. In architecture and design, form is closely coupled with geometry: position, orientation, size, proportion, and pattern. This studio explores the role of form not only in the construction of objects and space, but also in the construction of drawings and images.

The studio pedagogy is intended to advance representational skills, introduce new tools for managing complexity, and expand design vocabularies. Over the course of the studio, the design projects scale up progressively in size, intricacy, and complexity. "Scaling up" provides an entry point for exploring fundamental architectural problems such as tolerance, fidelity, and resolution.

Computer-aided design (CAD) software is introduced this semester as a new tool for drawing and modeling. Students are encouraged to develop expertise, as greater proficiency expands design possibilities, reduces production time, and promotes a deeper understanding of the role of form in architecture and design.

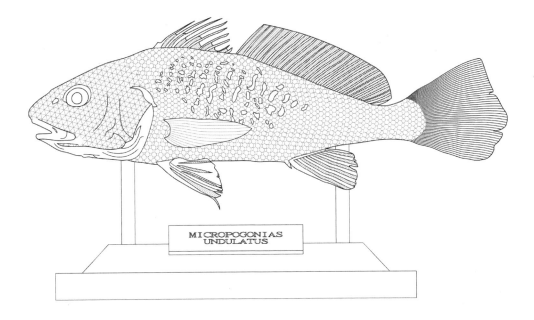

MICROPOGONIAS
UNDULATUS

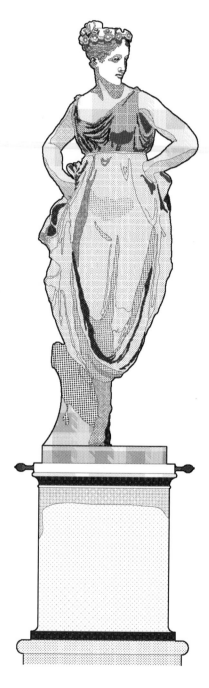

s> Kayleigh Macumber
s> Emily Brandt

i> Michael Crosby
i> Andrew Liles

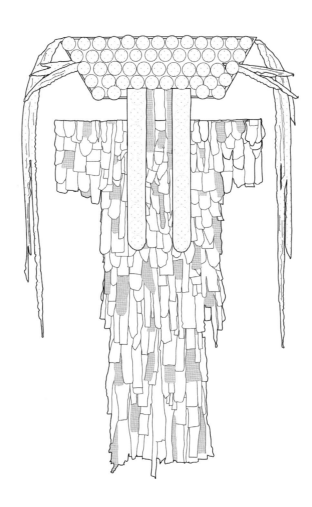

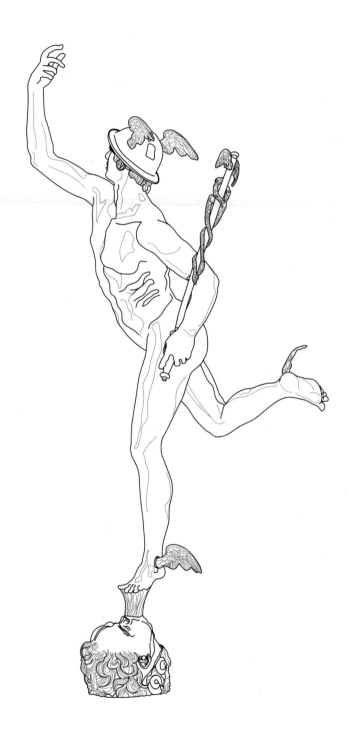

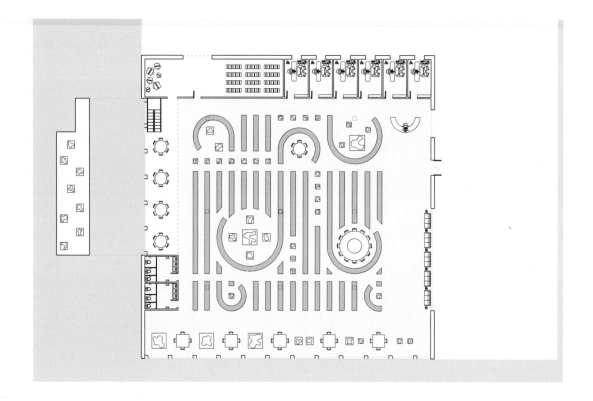

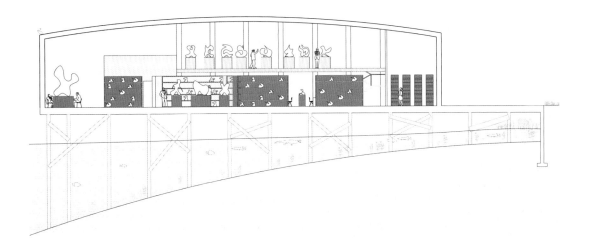

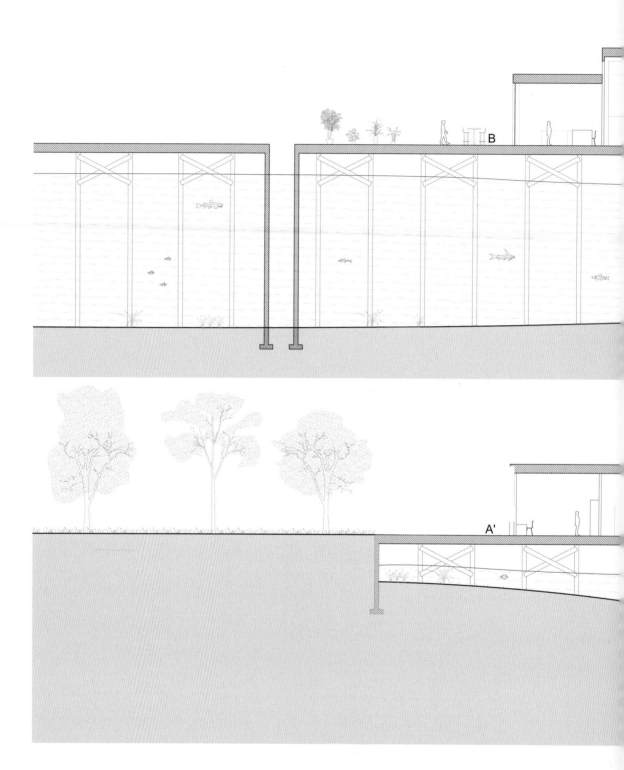

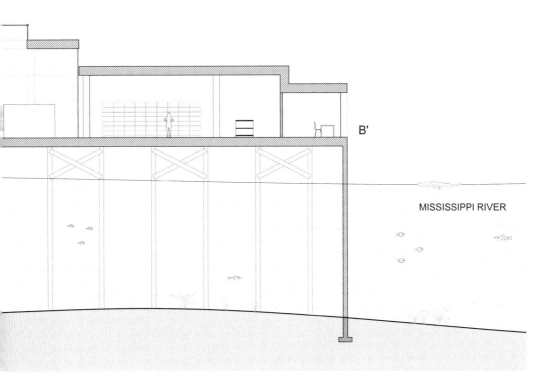

B'

MISSISSIPPI RIVER

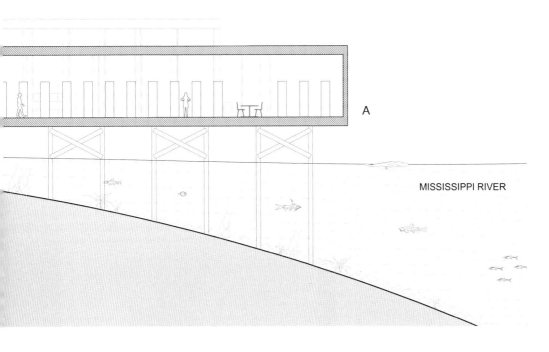

A

MISSISSIPPI RIVER

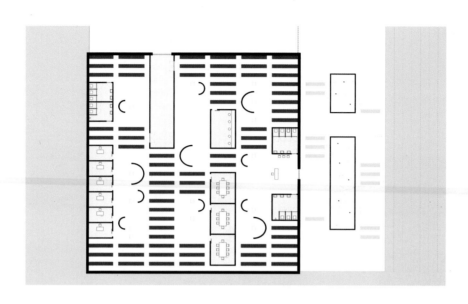

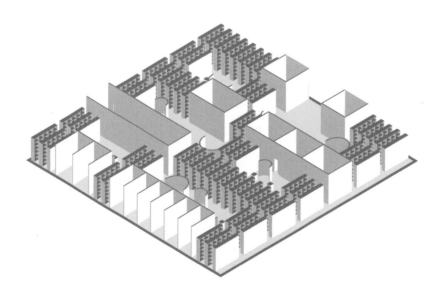

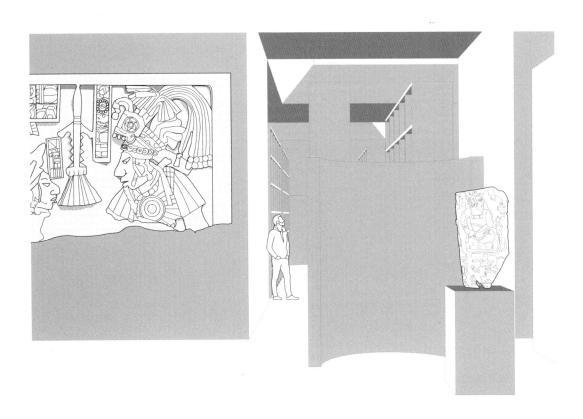

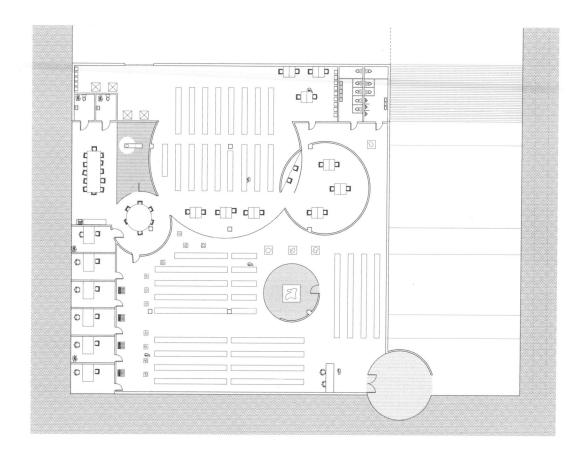

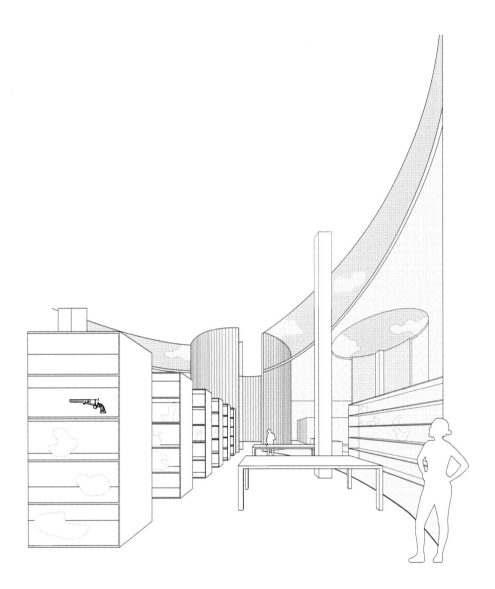

CONCEPTS AND PROGRAMS

Bardon de Tena [C]

ARCH 6011 -Culture- is the first half of a two-studio sequen-ce for the new graduate students enrolled in the summer courses. The main goal of the course is to help new students build the foundational skills of design and graphic processes and to learn the nature of studio work. This becomes the first step of the largest goal during their three-and-a-half year program: to become "visual thinkers" who transform their ideas into spatial organizations.

Through the analysis and transformation of a case study, the students explore the relationship between concepts, spatial schemes, and programs. This process helps them unders-tand the importance of clarity on the architectural scheme, by working with the "front of the house" and "back of the house" in different typologies: one public museum or gallery and one private housing project.

By starting with a case study, each student goes through a process of extracting, abstracting, exploring, relocating, and re-programming, to arrive at their proposal integrated into the New Orleans urban grid. The use of diagrams, catalogs, 2D representation plans/sections/elevations, axonometric projections, and perspectives help them as they learn main representation strategies.

From public to private. From private to public.
From various contexts to the New Orleans urban grid.

The methodology encourages the class to develop proposals by using both general thinking — to work with clear ideas-and, specific thinking — to contextualize them on real con-text and needs.

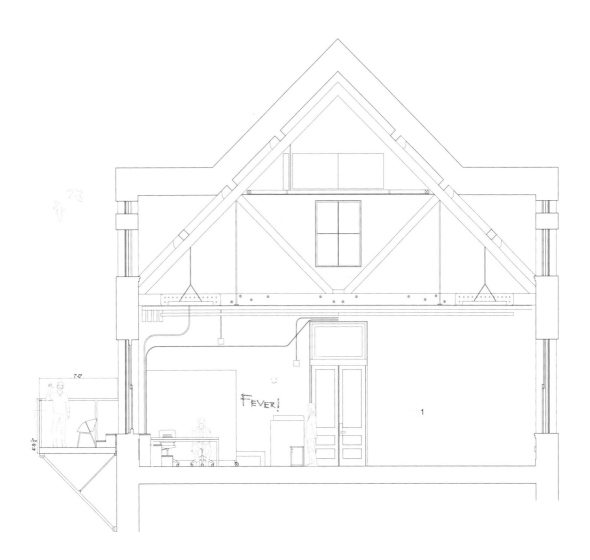

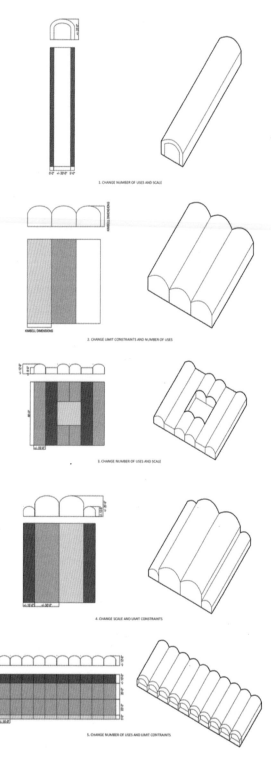

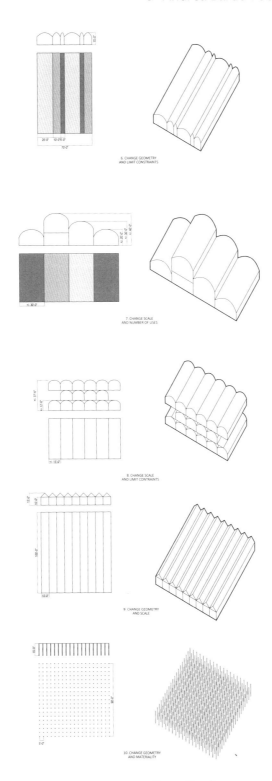

6. CHANGE GEOMETRY AND LIMIT CONSTRAINTS

7. CHANGE SCALE AND NUMBER OF USES

8. CHANGE SCALE AND LIMIT CONTRAINTS

9. CHANGE GEOMETRY AND SCALE

10. CHANGE GEOMETRY AND MATERIALITY

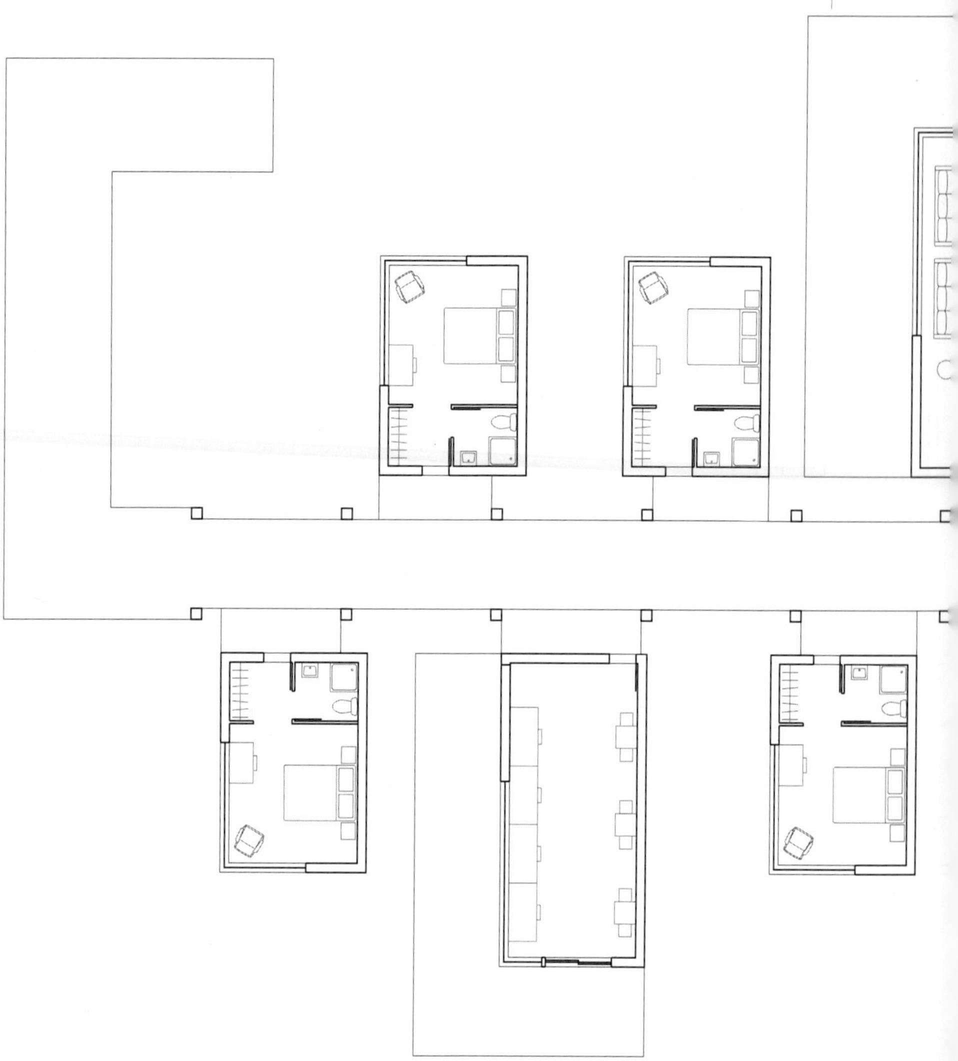

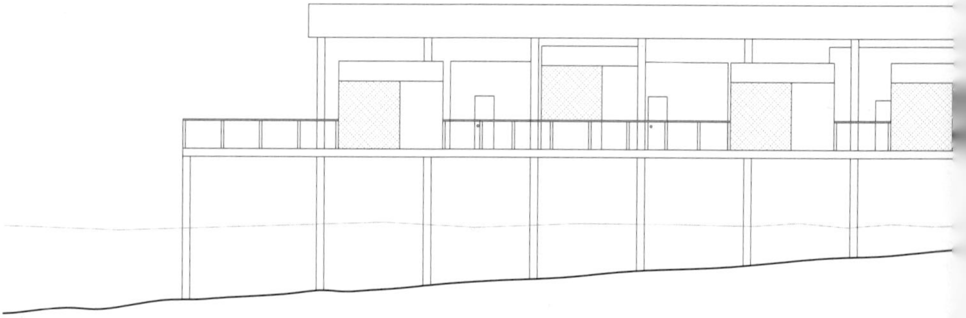

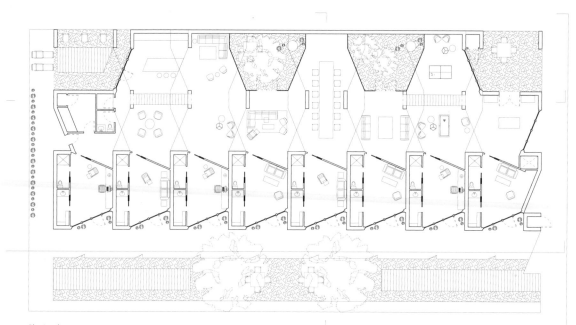

Plan Level 1

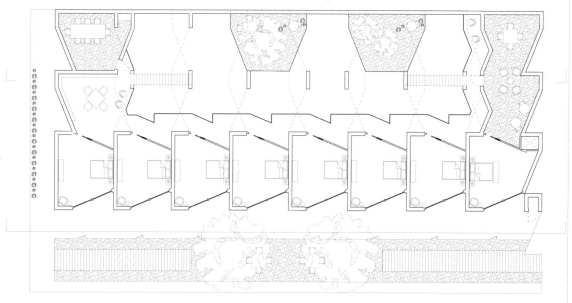

Plan Level 2

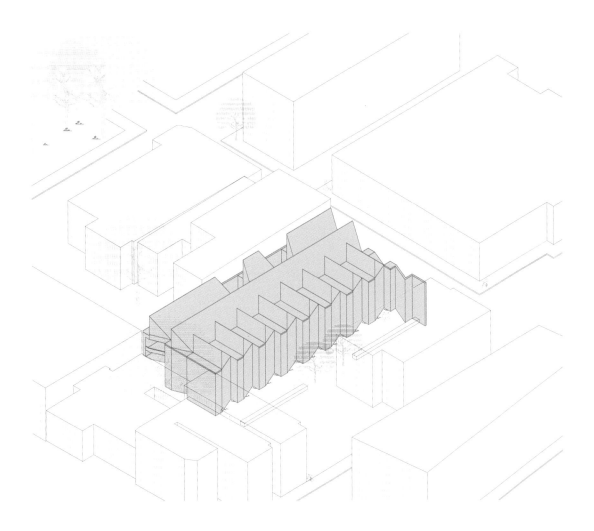

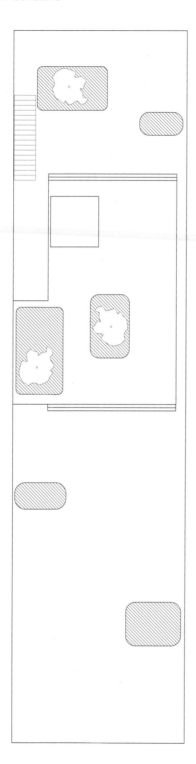
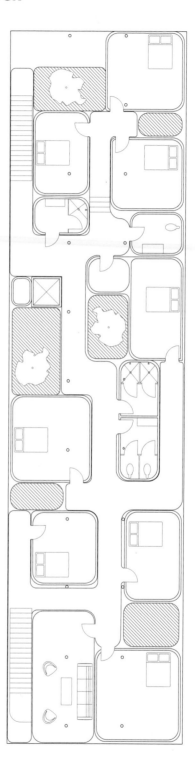

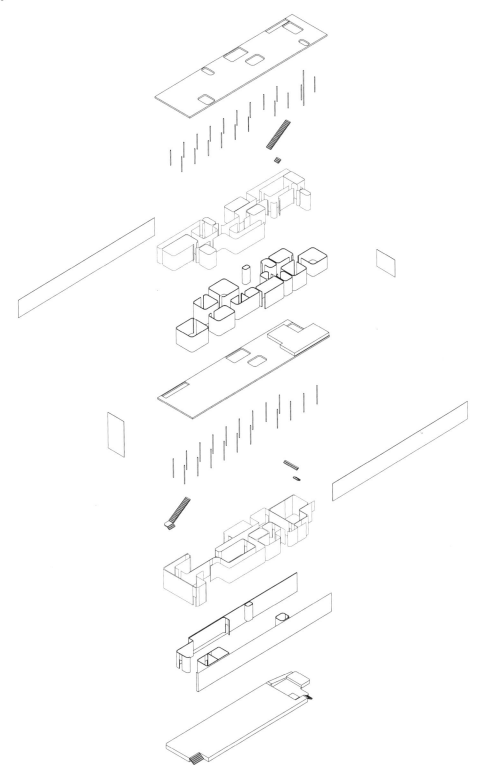

SITE AND CONSTRUCTION

Bardon de Tena [C]

ARCH 6012 -Materiality- is the second half of a two-studio sequence for the new graduate students enrolled in the summer courses.

The main goal of this course is to familiarize students with the construction systems, material properties, scale of structures, and create "visual thinkers". During this course, the students explore different representational scales: the territory scale, to analyze and understand the problems and challenges of the placement through mapping and the small scale, to explore the structural systems and construction details.

How can we think and design a space with materials and construction systems as a starting point?

The course takes the history of the Eames House — Case Study House No. 8, Los Angeles, 1949 — as a possible exercise hypothesis. Charles and Ray Eames, having the materials of their house already in place, decided to rethink their project and configure a different space with the same construction pieces. The students, over five weeks, found themselves in a similar situation.

In this case, we imagine that each student "lands" in a specific territory — a national park in the United States — with a load of materials from a building — a 20th-century case study. Students analyze the assigned case study, specifically its most significant materials and construction systems, to understand how they work and use its material in their project proposals: a shelter in nature.

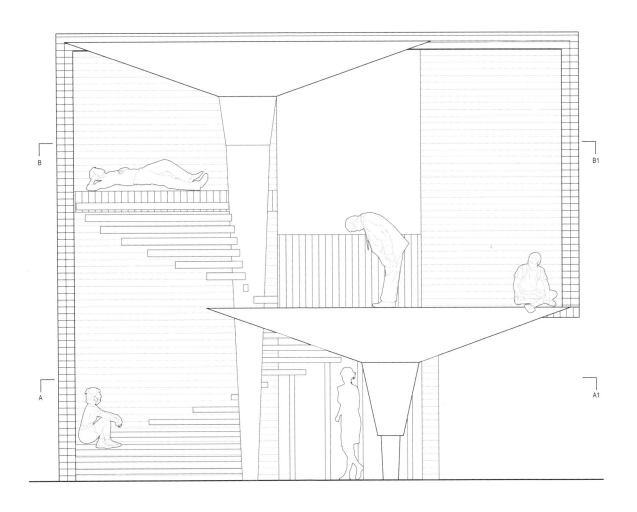

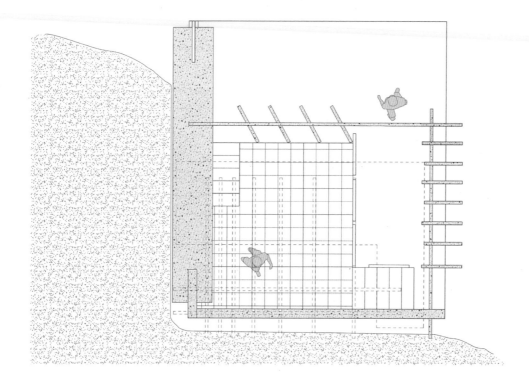

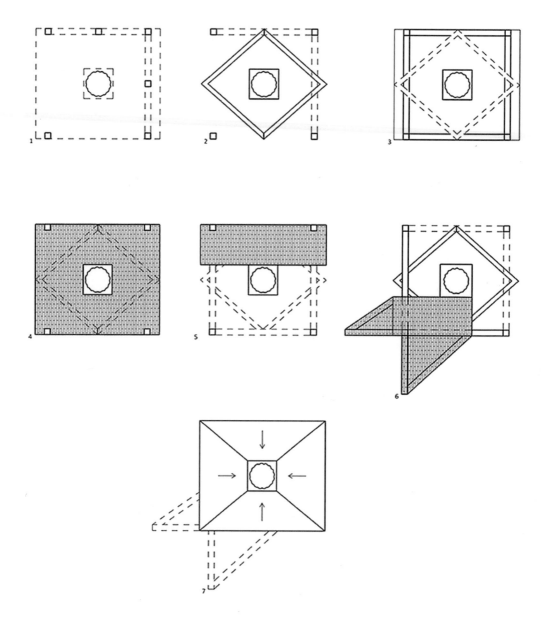

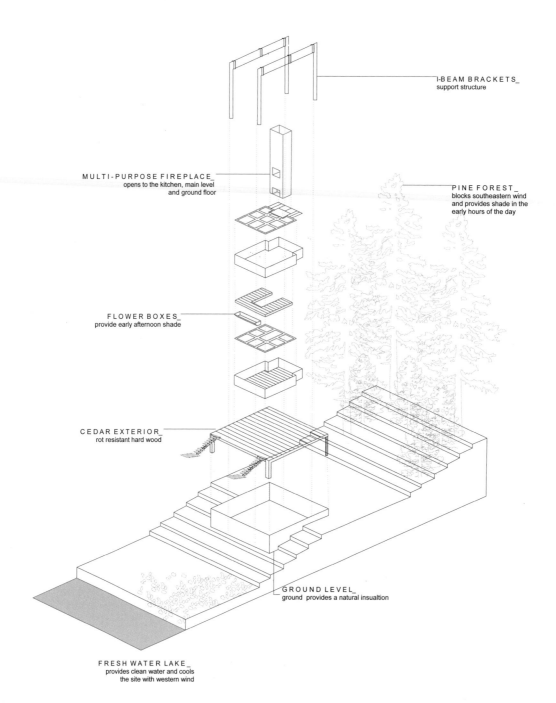

I-BEAM BRACKETS_
support structure

MULTI-PURPOSE FIREPLACE_
opens to the kitchen, main level
and ground floor

PINE FOREST_
blocks southeastern wind
and provides shade in the
early hours of the day

FLOWER BOXES_
provide early afternoon shade

CEDAR EXTERIOR_
rot resistant hard wood

GROUND LEVEL_
ground provides a natural insualtion

FRESH WATER LAKE_
provides clean water and cools
the site with western wind

s> Ryan Russell
s> Elliot Slovis

i> Andrea Bardon de Tena
i> Andrea Bardon de Tena

BUILDING & LANDSCAPE

Kinnard [C]
Lin | Redfield | Roser Gray | Lockhart

This studio focuses on the role of the landscape in architectural design and the development of basic skills in site analysis, site design, and site representation. Site characteristics are to be understood as both natural — a result of the actions of nature — and cultural — a result of the actions of people.

Students are introduced to a range of conceptual strategies for articulating the relationship between building and site, developing the ability to sculpt the surface of the land to accommodate human activities.

The course highlights the designer's ethical obligations to the larger network of social and ecological systems and conditions. Building design themes include spatial organization and hierarchy, circulation, structure, and enclosure. The studio is integrated with digital media classes to ensure that students gain fluency in computer-aided design processes, drawing, spatial modeling, and digital design techniques.

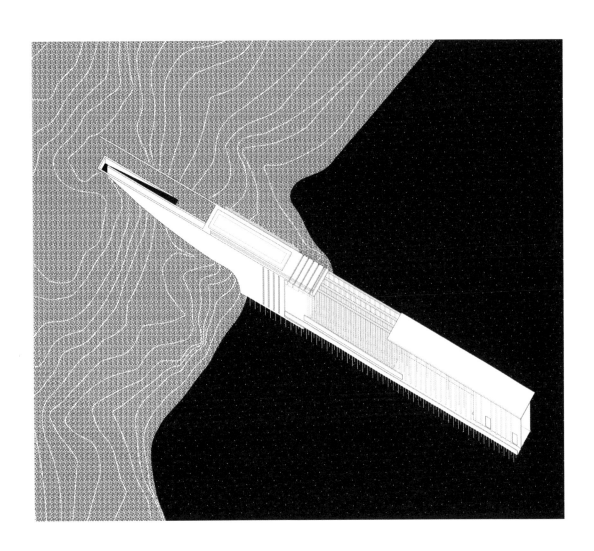

s> Chase Isget
s> William Trotter

i> Cordula Roser Gray
i> Tiffany Lin

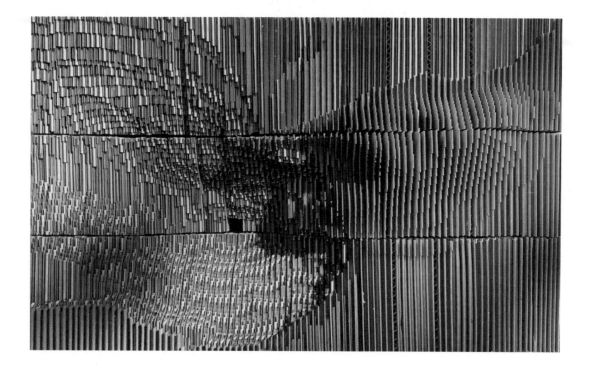

s> Chelsea Kilgore
s> Sarie Keller

i> Tiffany Lin
i> Judith Kinnard

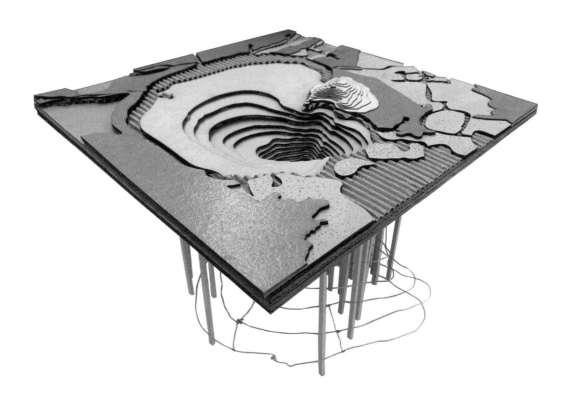

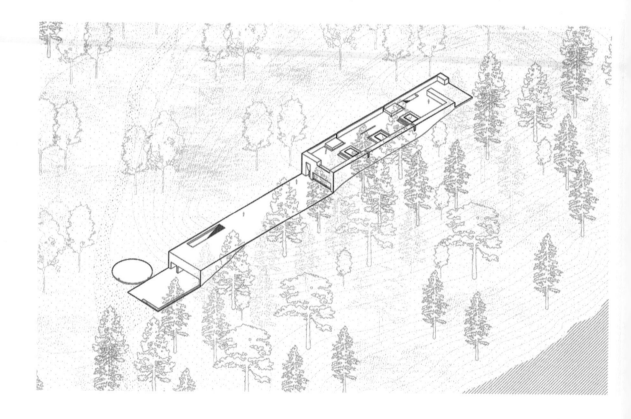

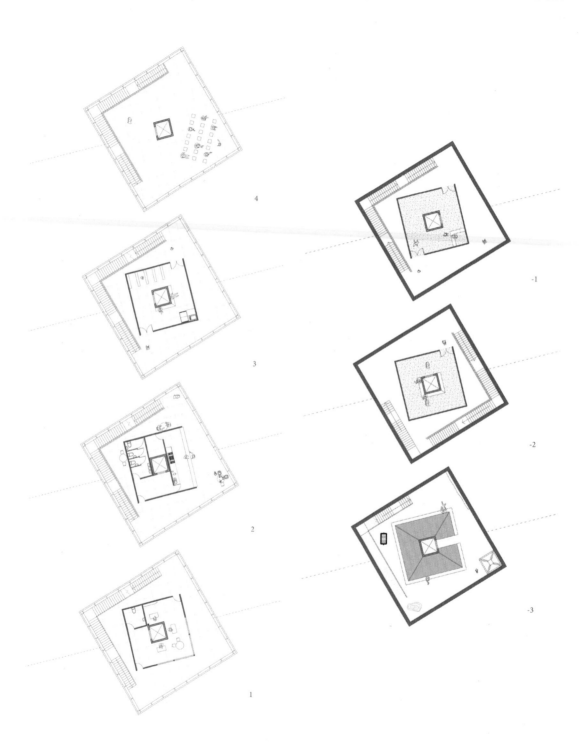

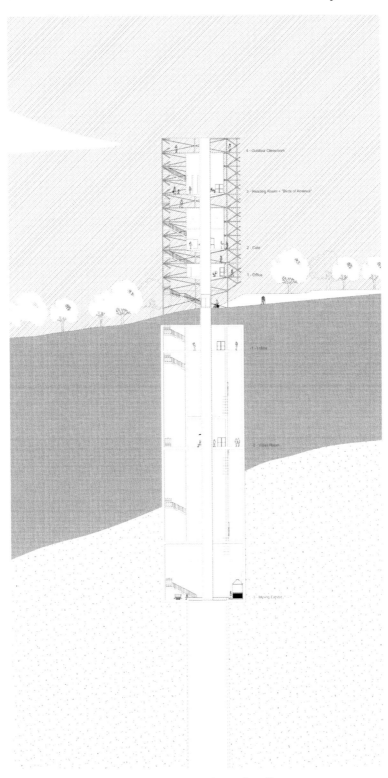

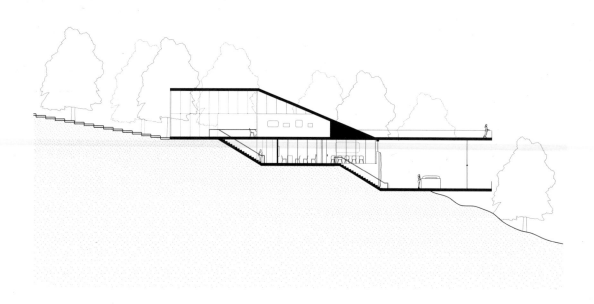

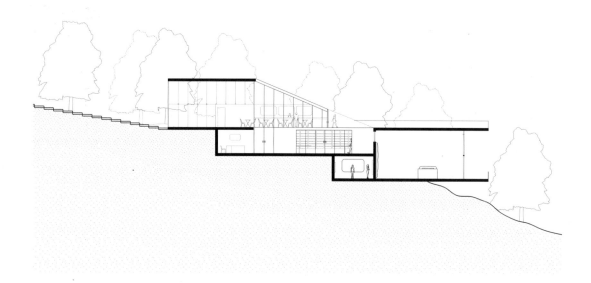

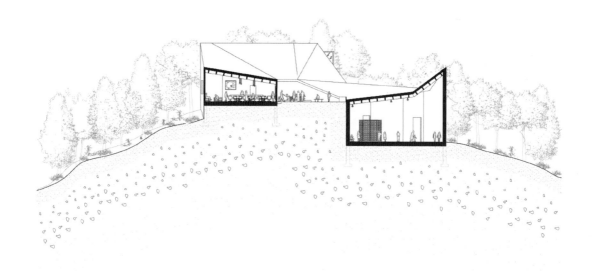

COLLECTIVE HOUSING

Jover [C]

Norman | Vela | Lockhart | Bardon de Tena

The main object of design in this studio is collective housing. However, it is an atypical collective housing. It is a composite of homes of different sizes with collective amenities and collective grounds. This course raises the question of whether collective housing can be considered in the regime of "intentional communities".

When a community of ~20 owners on site hypothetically decide to redevelop their land, they hire an architect to design their dream and ask themselves: how would we like to live together? When densifying the urban block, each owner will have three to five homes, instead of one. Each owner will have the advantages and assets of the American suburban home — large open space, amenities — but in a regime of shared ownership, and in a more compact and ecologically minded way. This transformation will allow the larger collective grounds to be used for anything from orchards to water management to sports, etc. Later in the semester, three owners within the urban block decide to stay in their old houses; these parcels and homes will have to be respected on site.

The pedagogy starts with a drawing exercise of an extremely small space of inhabitation — a boat or an airstream — followed by a sequence of short projects that are the horizontal patio home, the vertical home, and the sectional home. The remaining seven weeks are dedicated to recombining the previous projects to design 60-100 homes for an urban block where three owners decide to stay. As part of the site analysis, students draw plans and sections of domestic porches along a given street in New Orleans.

Current condition of the block

Buildings to maintain

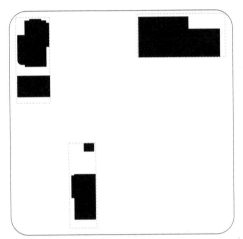

Possible collective housing strategy

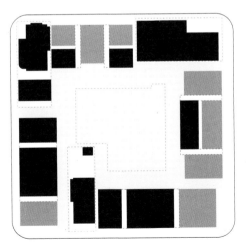

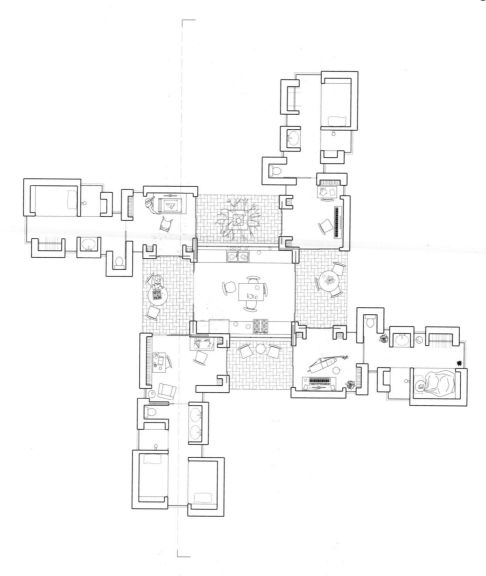

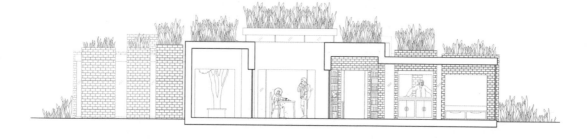

s> Ian Shaw
s> Anna Kathryn Becker

i> Carrie Norman
i> Sonsoles Vela

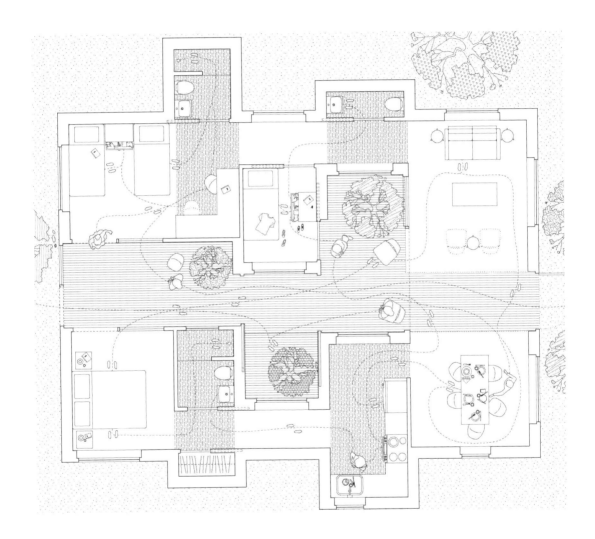

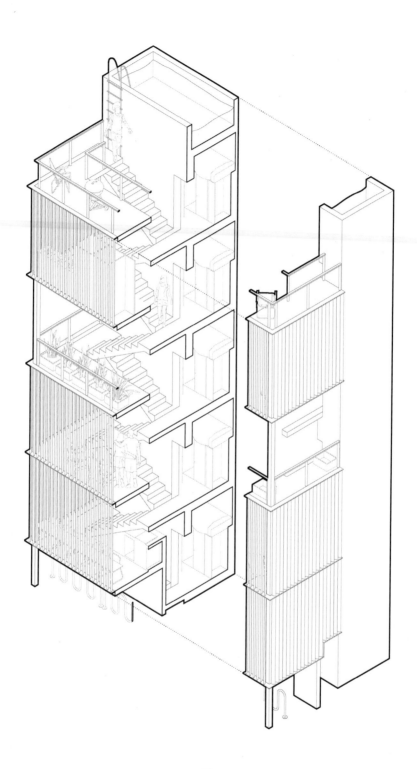

s> Jose Varela Castillo
s> Chelsea Kilgore

i> Carrie Norman
i> Andrea Bardon de Tena

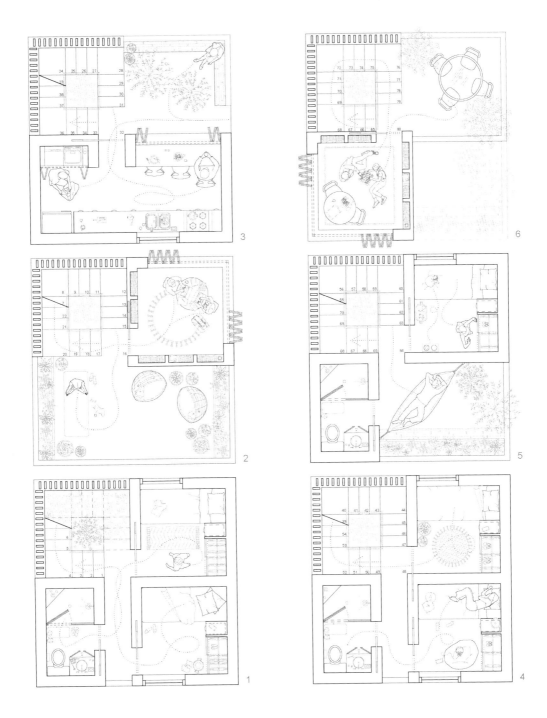

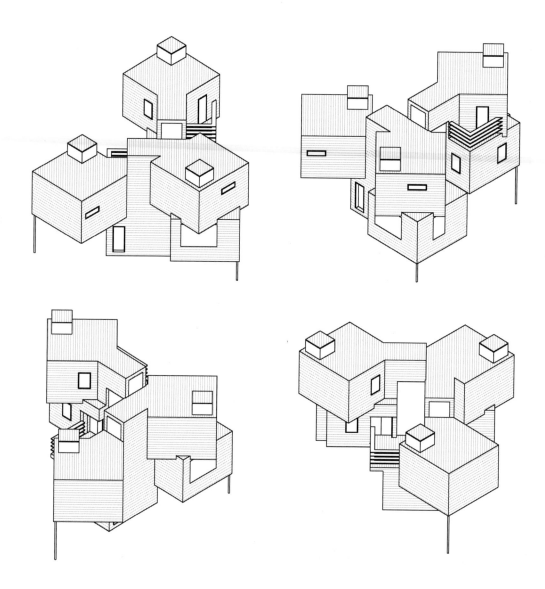

s> Tom O'Brien
s> Jake Davis

i> Margarita Jover
i> Andrea Bardon de Tena

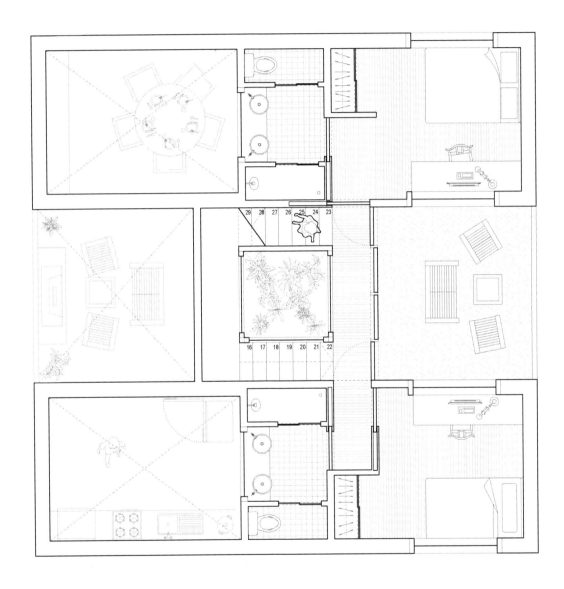

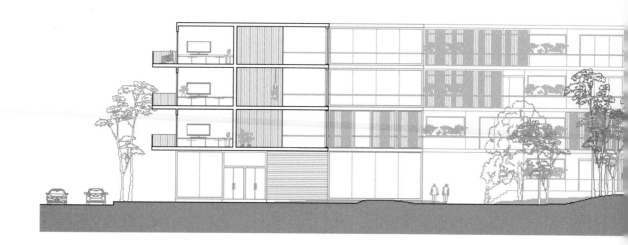

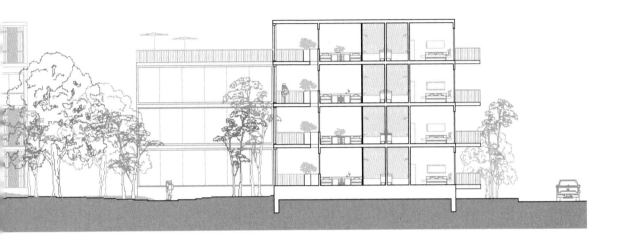

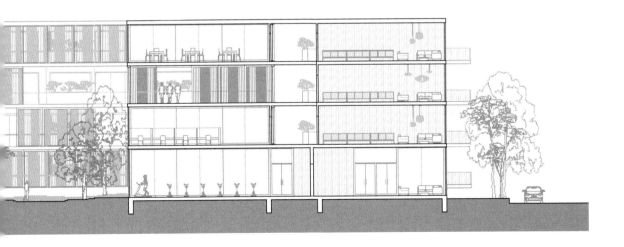

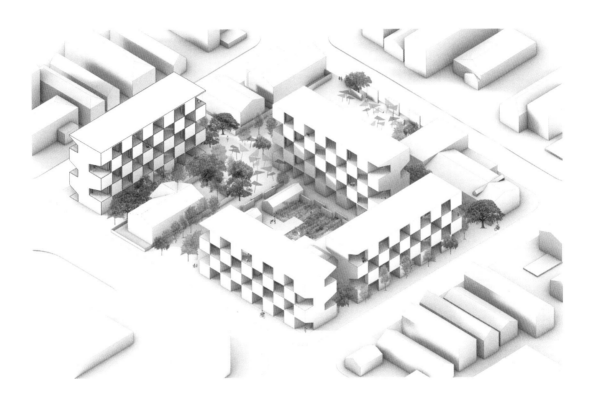

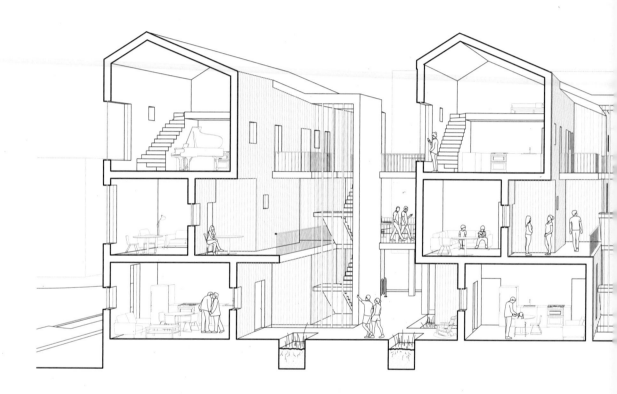

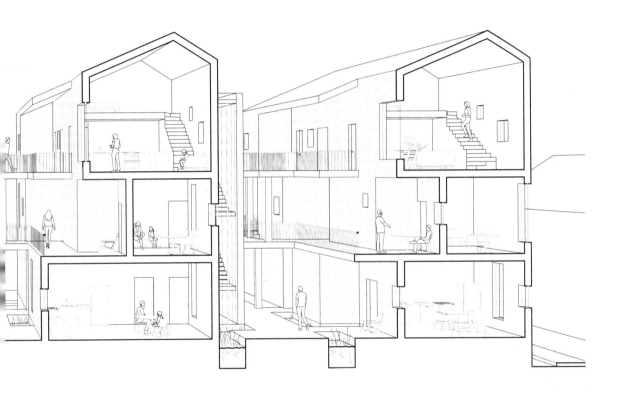

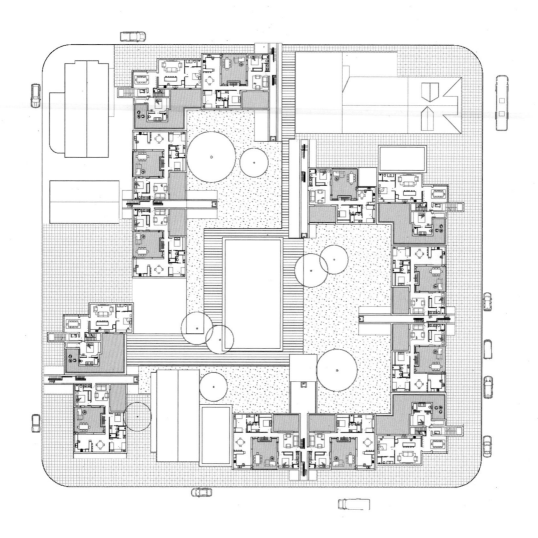

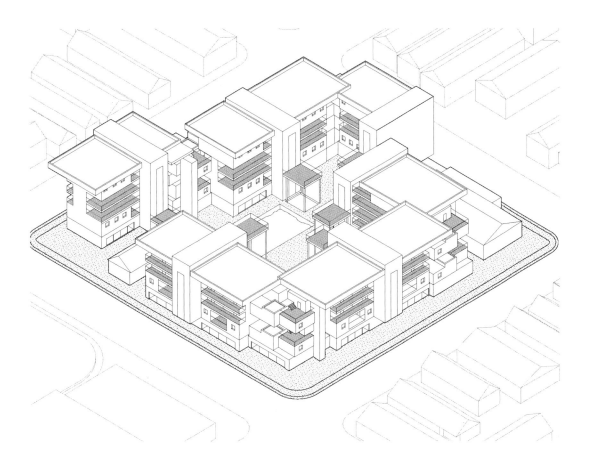

NEW ORLEANS SCENARIOS FOR A RESILIENT NEIGHBORHOOD

Keil [C]
Goodwin | Vela

The 3031 architecture design studio introduces students to the scale of the city — reinforcing and expanding the previously learned lessons of building organization and program circulation within a city block to larger areas of the city.

Students are introduced to the vocabulary and the instruments of urban design; they investigate and analyze/map the urban context at various scales; they research and analyze precedents; they synthesize their findings and, in an urban scenario emphasizing sustainable density and water resiliency, speculate on the development of a series of parcels with respect to context, program, zoning parameters, and site opportunities. In a further development phase, the strategies laid out in this urban plan are the basis for the detailed design of a particular building on the site.

The studio project is structured in two phases. In Phase I, Urban Scale, students establish a conceptual scenario for the development of the site (group work in student teams).

In Phase II, Building Scale, students design a building in more detail with the urban scenario as a basis (individual work).

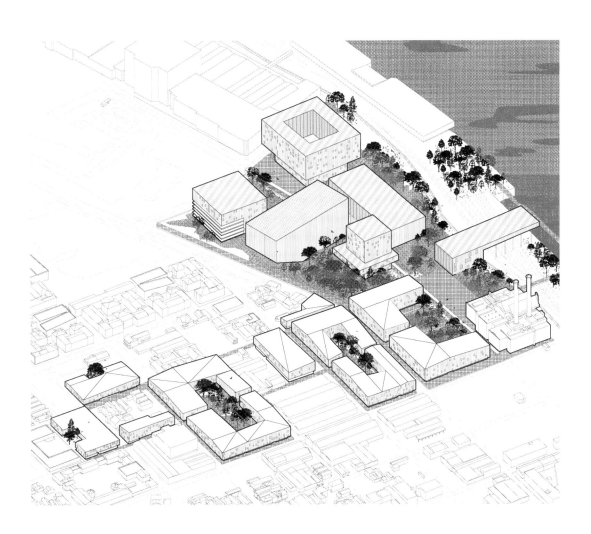

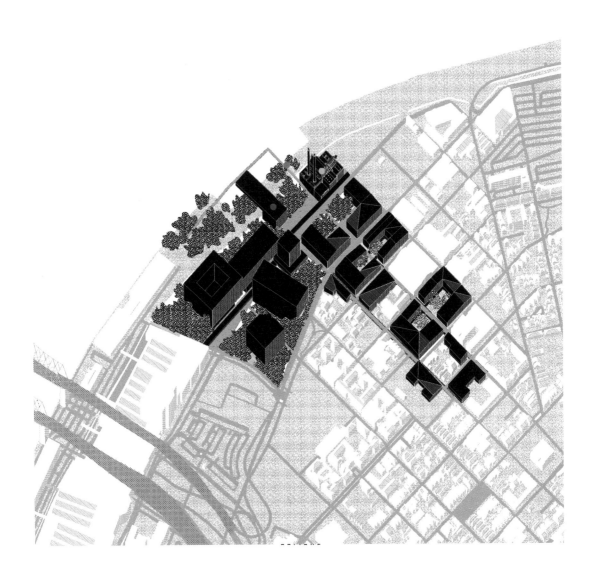

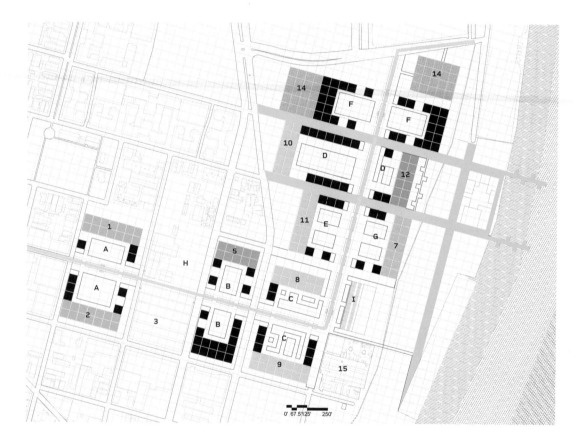

1. Food Court
2. Grocery Store
3. Market
4. Restaurants
5. Gym
6. Coworking Spaces
7. Apartments
8. Gallery
9. Resilience Center
10. Museum
11. Theater
12. Hotel
13. Offices
14. Parking
15. Renewable Energy

A. Urban Farm
B. Skate Park
C. Sculpture Park
D. Outdoor Food Hall
E. Aquaponics
F. Event Park
G. Pool
H. Outdoor Sports Center
I. Open Air Theater

s> Sam Spencer, Avanti Patel, Mitchell Lyons **i>** Sonsoles Vela

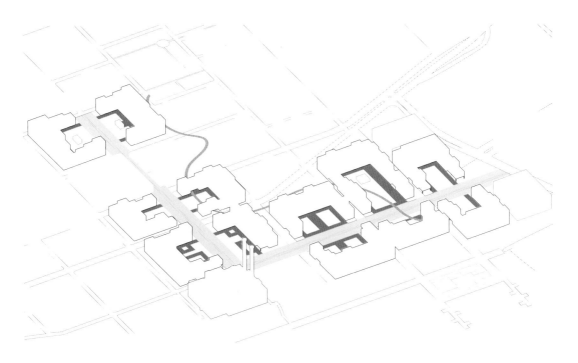

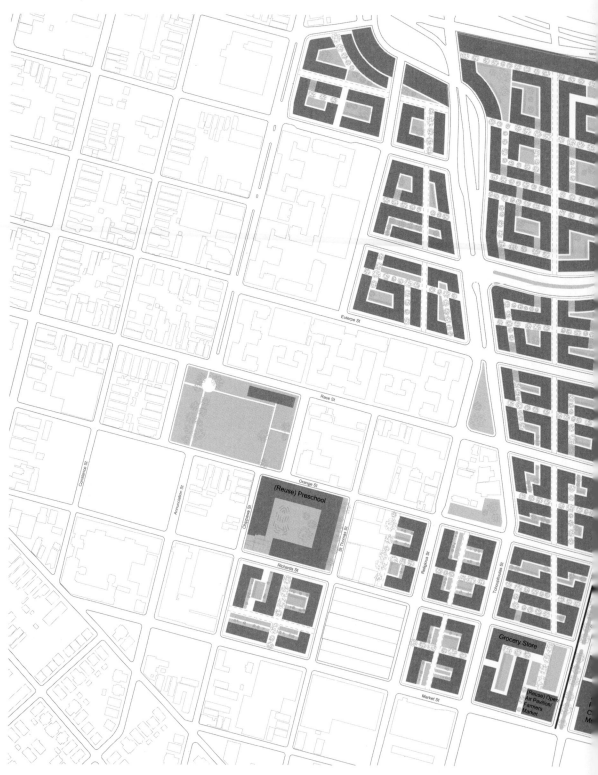

s> Clara Gardner, Olivia Georgakopoulos   **i>** Bruce Goodwin

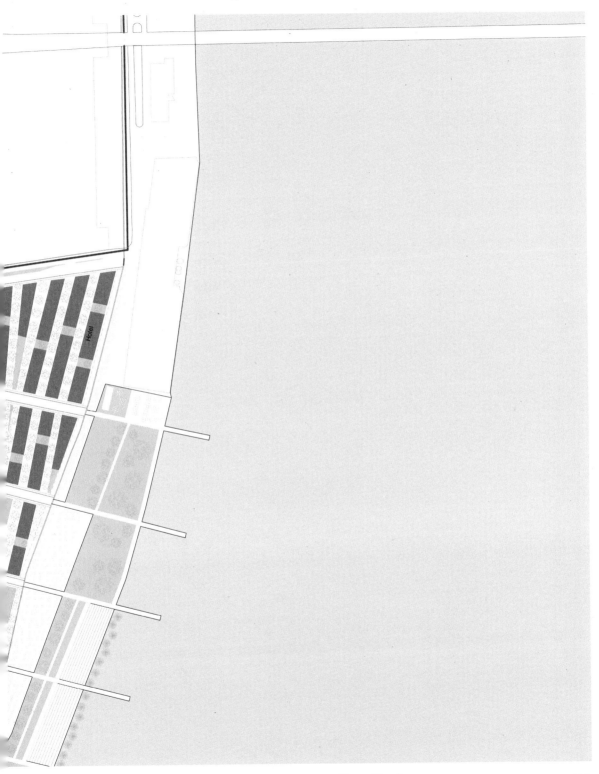

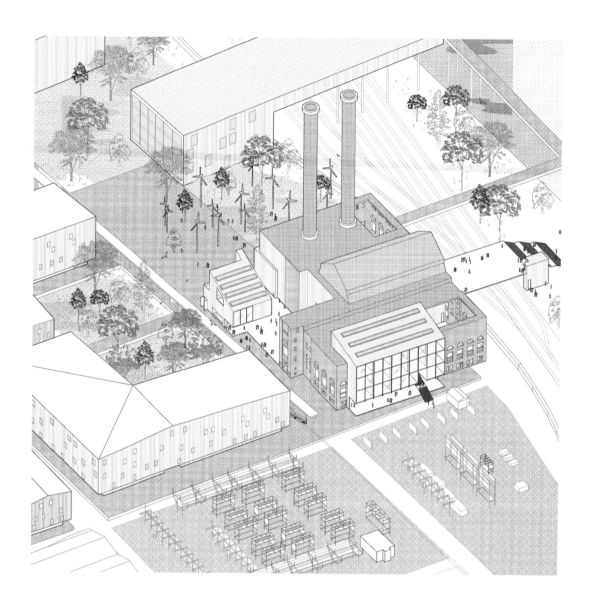

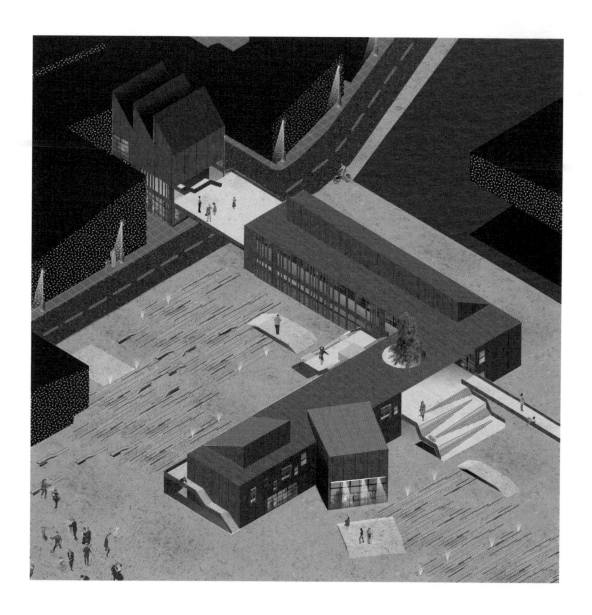

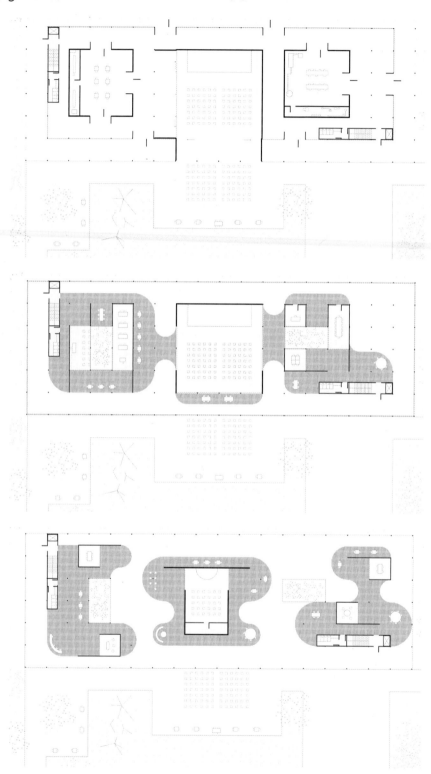

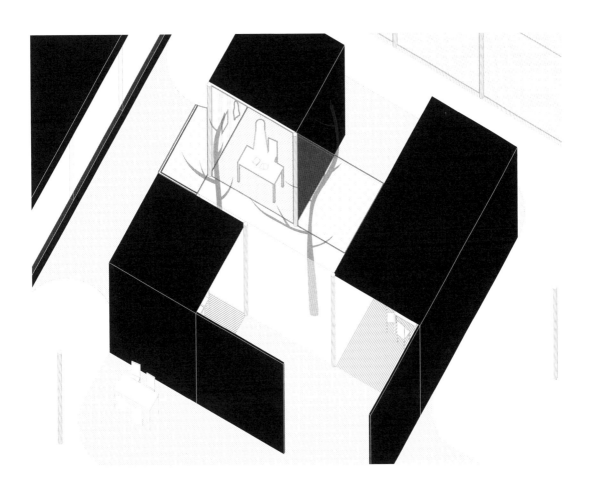

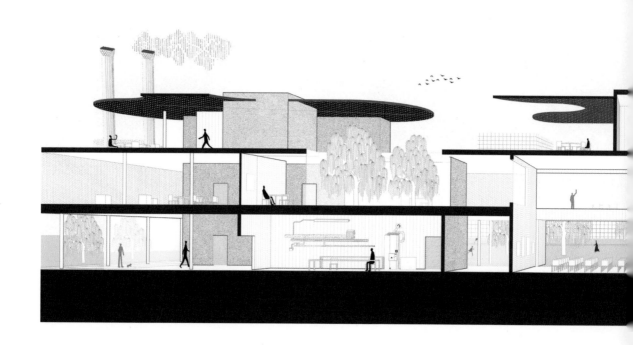

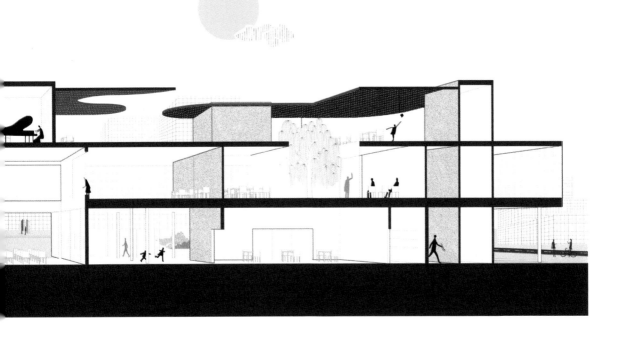

INTEGRATED DESIGN STUDIO

Keil [C]
Garcia-Rubio | Goodwin | Hattori | Taylor-Welty

This studio focuses on the development of an architectural project with regards to site relationships, historic context, structure, systems, materiality, and building codes, meeting the NAAB accreditation requirements of the integrated studio. "Integration" is understood not only as a coordination of building systems during the project development, but also as a constant reciprocal feedback between intent and material manifestation — a careful calibration of intent, form, system, material, and technology where relationships are never unidirectional, but have inherent potentials and unanticipated possibilities.

The pedagogical objective of this studio is to lead the student through a design process in which architectural ideas, spatial planning, and building technologies are integrated. Students are expected to understand and comply with all applicable building code regulations, such as life safety and egress. The implications of construction techniques, building technologies, and systems are addressed and explored in this course.

The project is a mixed-use building on an infill site. Students work individually on one design project over the semester. The office component is divided into a space occupied by a specific client and rentable work/studio spaces. The studio uses a hypothetical scenario that PROSPECT NEW ORLEANS, a citywide contemporary art triennial, will be moving their administrative headquarters to a location in the Warehouse District. The building will house their offices and community outreach spaces on street level, but also provide lease spaces for associated creative agencies and individuals co-working spaces above.

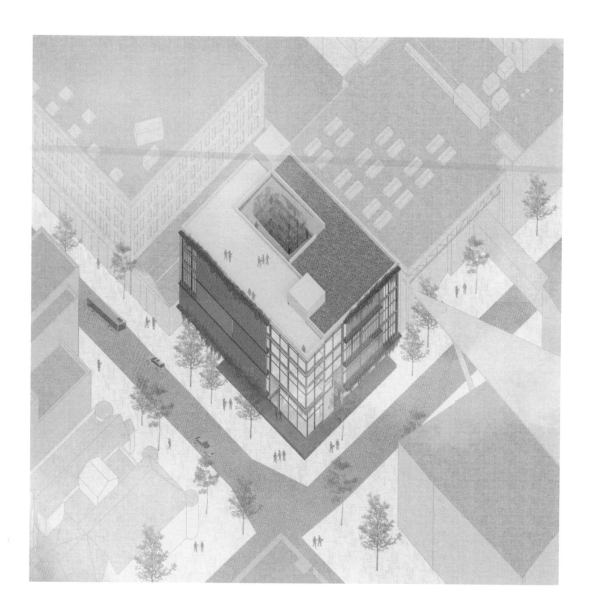

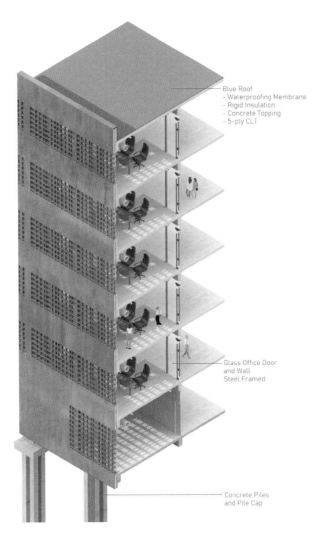

Blue Roof
- Waterproofing Membrane
- Rigid Insulation
- Concrete Topping
- 5-ply CLT

Glass Office Door
and Wall
Steel Framed

Concrete Piles
and Pile Cap

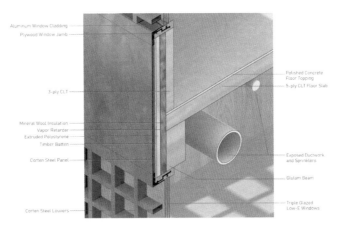

Aluminum Window Cladding

Plywood Window Jamb

Polished Concrete
Floor Topping

5-ply CLT Floor Slab

3-ply CLT

Mineral Wool Insulation

Vapor Retarder

Extruded Polystyrene

Timber Batten

Corten Steel Panel

Exposed Ductwork
and Sprinklers

Glulam Beam

Triple Glazed
Low-E Windows

Corten Steel Louvers

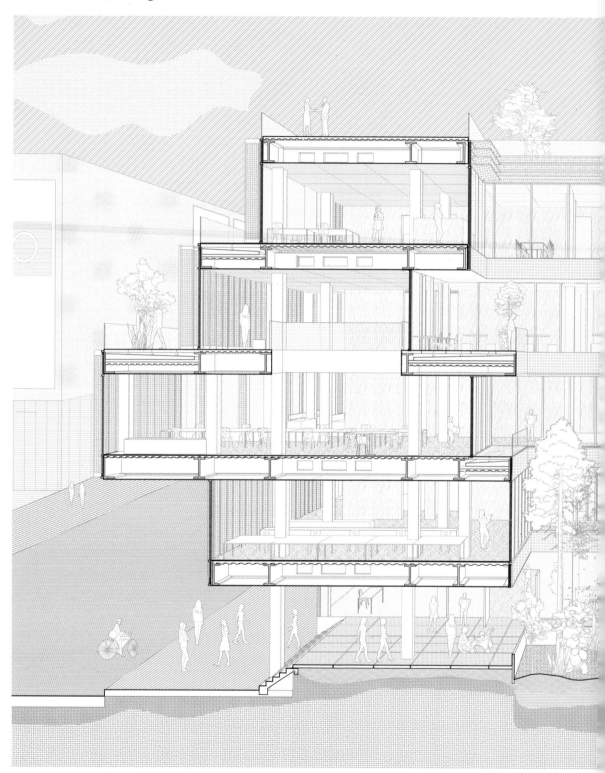

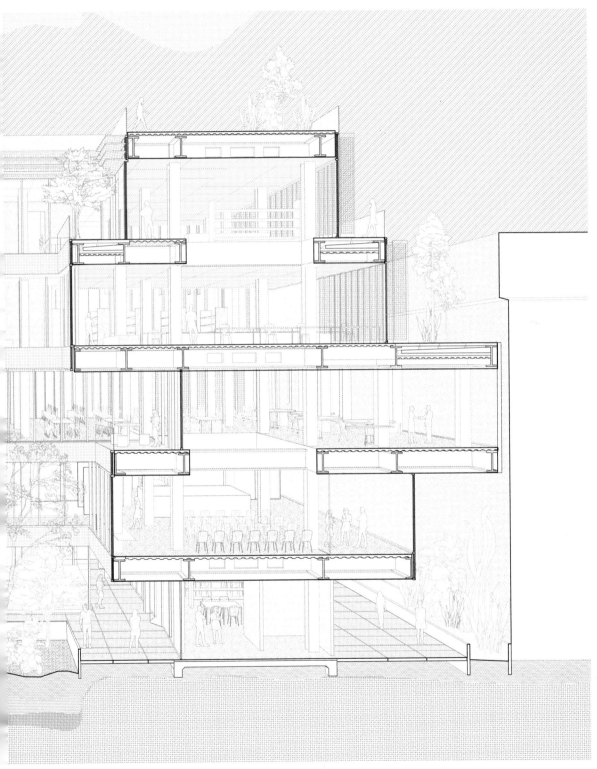

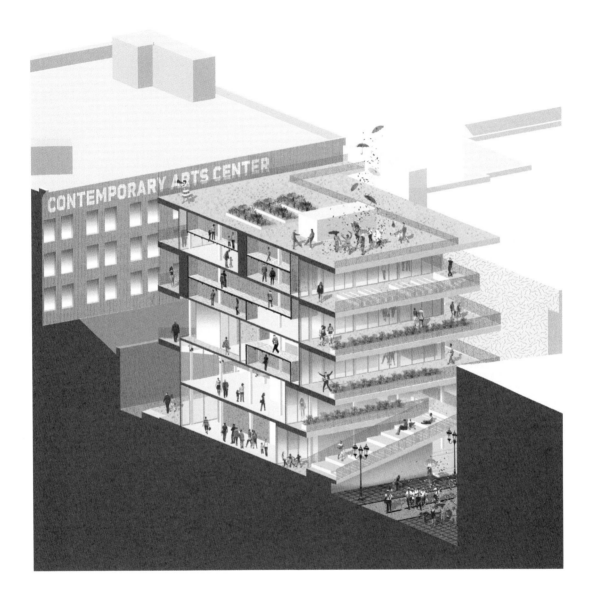

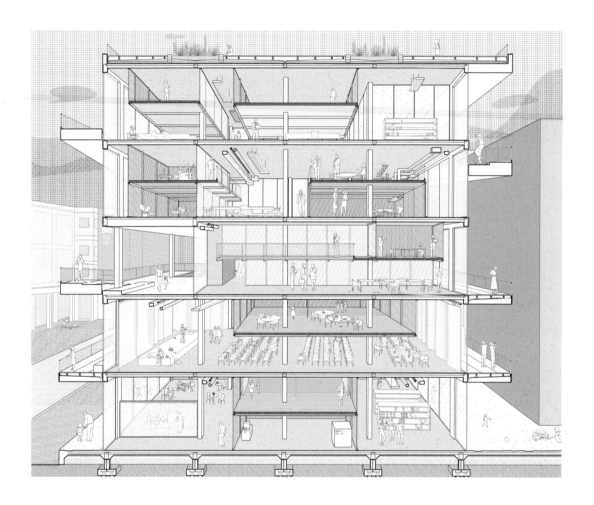

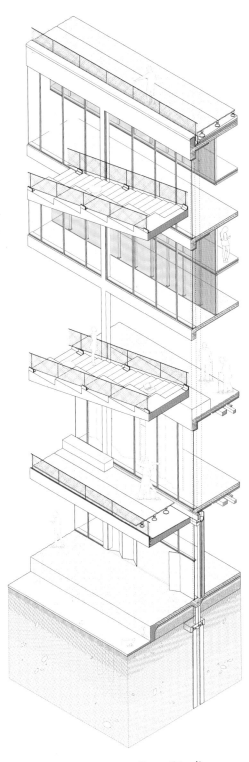

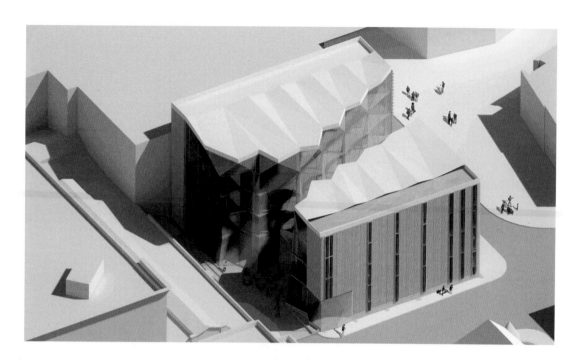

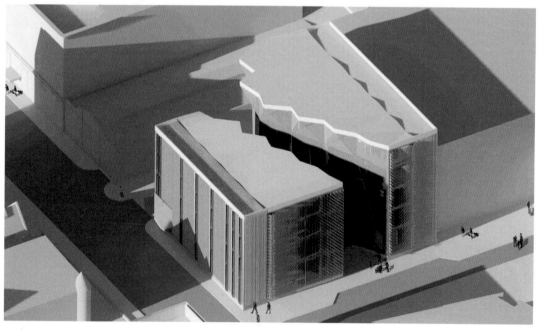

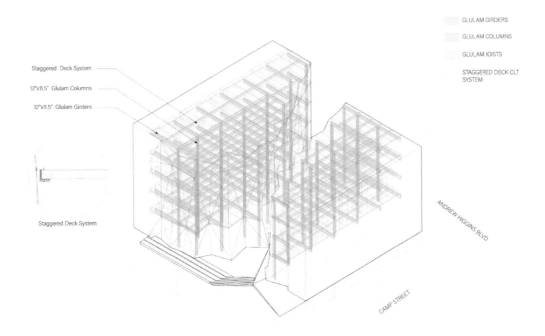

Staggered Deck System

12"x11.5" Glulam Columns

12"x11.5" Glulam Girders

Staggered Deck System

GLULAM GIRDERS

GLULAM COLUMNS

GLULAM JOISTS

STAGGERED DECK CLT SYSTEM

ANDREW HIGGINS BLVD

CAMP STREET

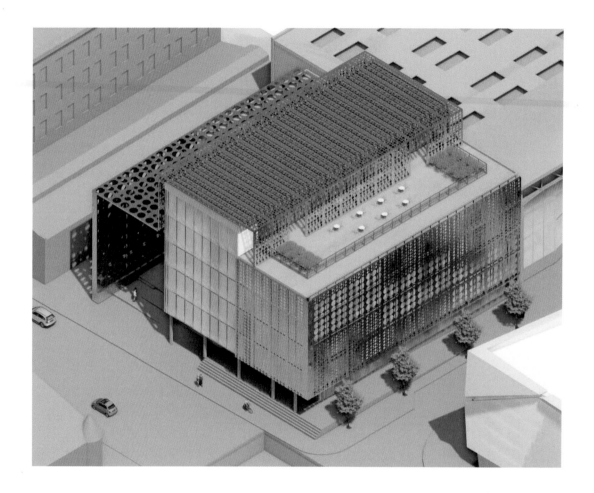

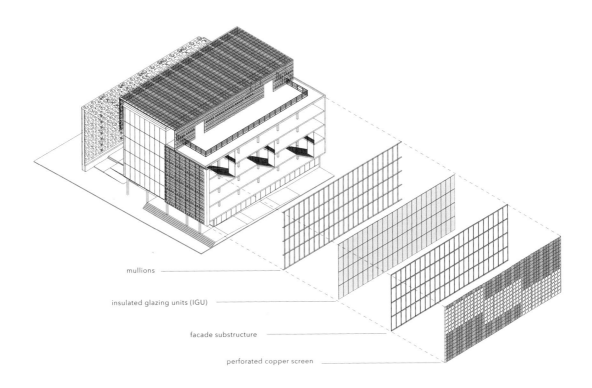

mullions ———————————

insulated glazing units (IGU) ———————————

facade substructure ———————————

perforated copper screen ———————————

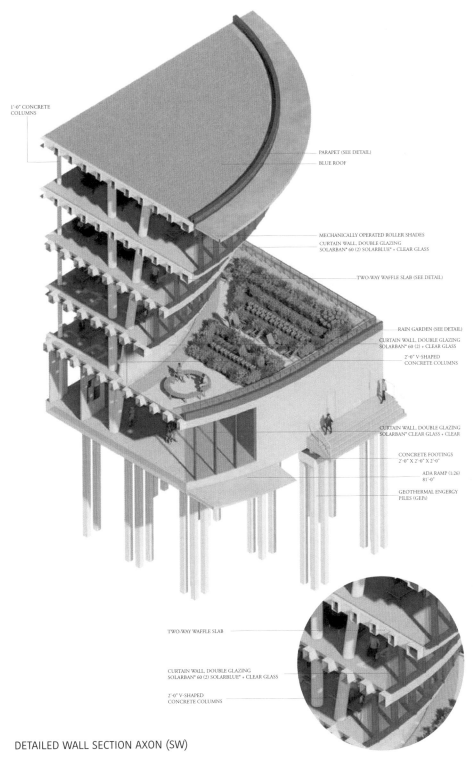

1'-0" CONCRETE
COLUMNS

PARAPET (SEE DETAIL)
BLUE ROOF

MECHANICALLY OPERATED ROLLER SHADES
CURTAIN WALL, DOUBLE GLAZING
SOLARBAN® 60 (2) SOLARBLUE® + CLEAR GLASS

TWO-WAY WAFFLE SLAB (SEE DETAIL)

RAIN GARDEN (SEE DETAIL)
CURTAIN WALL, DOUBLE GLAZING
SOLARBAN® 60 (2) + CLEAR GLASS

2'-0" V-SHAPED
CONCRETE COLUMNS

CURTAIN WALL, DOUBLE GLAZING
SOLARBAN® CLEAR GLASS + CLEAR

CONCRETE FOOTINGS
2'-0" X 2'-0" X 2'-0"

ADA RAMP (1:26)
81'-0"

GEOTHERMAL ENGERGY
PILES (GEPs)

TWO-WAY WAFFLE SLAB

CURTAIN WALL, DOUBLE GLAZING
SOLARBAN® 60 (2) SOLARBLUE® + CLEAR GLASS

2'-0" V-SHAPED
CONCRETE COLUMNS

DETAILED WALL SECTION AXON (SW)

Scott Bernhard

Associate Dean for Academics

A New History Course Concept at TuSA

Beginning in the spring of 2021, the School of Architecture's Graduate and Undergraduate history courses were reconfigured into a series of half-semester "mini-courses;" each of which begins with a contemporary figure in architectural practice and proceeds in a reverse chronology to explore the precedents and linages of architectural thought that have been synthesized in the work of that contemporary practice. We have chosen four such figures of contemporary practice as *key points of departure* to examine a range of architectural origins and influences. Teaching by example, these courses will offer a lesson in precedent research methods and equip students to apply such procedures on their own in subsequent design and research work. The instructors of these "mini-courses" teach a seven-week segment twice in the semester, to graduate and undergraduate groups. Much of the course material is the same from the graduate to the undergraduate versions, but the delivery methods and course products vary to suit the student group.

Received Traditions and Conventional History/ Theory Education in Architecture

The standard or traditional form of architectural history instruction often begins with some form of historical survey with canonical examples and significant architectural achievements. These valuable elements of the historical framework are often presented in a chronological sequence that creates a backdrop for later elaboration and deeper exploration. This continuum of typically western (or mostly western) architectural periods is now, more commonly, punctuated with parallel or contrary developments in non-western contexts. This method presents some diversity of architectural activity through time but tends to be presented from a western *point of reference* and is measured, implicitly, relative to western norms.

Likewise, this standard survey sequence is offered beginning with origins in the distant past (often ancient Egypt or pre-history) and moves forward through two or three semesters to a roughly contemporary moment and an engagement of present-day practice. Placing the most immediately relevant portions of a survey at the end of a long sequence often presents challenges to the relative utility of the material in the early courses, since they commonly deal with subjects, technologies, and societies long discontinued. The early portions of chronological surveys can sometimes seem more like archaeology than architecture per se.

After a foundational series of survey courses, most programs offer advanced courses in architectural history and theory that are narrower in focus — often predicated on a basic historical framework acquired in the survey courses. The idea has been that a broad frame of reference comes first and then areas of depth are developed through small seminar-formatted coursework.

Obviously, this form of architectural education is valuable and there are many useful points of reference communicated through this treatment of history and through this time-honored teaching method. As well, it should be said that our previous "survey sequence" at TuSA was *more complex and richly configured than the generic examples described above.* This new method is not intended to replace a "broken" or "dis-functional" system or unsuccessful faculty efforts. However, some of the objections (implicit in the descriptions above) have made us question the norm and the premise of our modified survey-based courses. Many fields have abandoned or dramatically altered their survey teaching in the past twenty years, and we hope that a refreshed approach will help us to engage a new array of ambitions described below. In January of 2020, the Art History Department of Yale University announced the dissolution of their Art History survey courses — seeking to ensure that a "diversity of research and resources can inform and energize our teaching" and student learning outcomes (Art Forum, February 2020). We are seeking a teaching method and schema that will foreground contemporary issues in architectural theory and practice; and a system that aims to identify useful linkages between the past and present.

Ambitions and Objectives

If the great examples of architecture from the past could be compared to brightly colored fish, we seek a system of History/Theory education that teaches "fishing method" rather than merely offering the fascinating fish themselves. In this way, we hope our students become accomplished researchers, able to connect a useful taxonomy of architectural examples to contemporary issues and ambitions. We want our students to see the cannon as a wide and open pool with unexpected richness and useful links to the present. Thus, we propose to teach history and theory in architecture in a reverse chronology, moving from *points of departure* in the present (or recent) world of architectural practice to the more distant antecedents that have supported and continue to inform the discipline today. As with our previous history/theory courses, we seek learning outcomes in research methods, architectural analysis, and critical thinking.

Recognizing that any point of departure tends to influence the trajectory of a search, we propose increasing these points, represented in each instructor's expertise, to four from two. Four instructors will teach a seven-week course segment to graduate and undergraduate course sections in sequence. Thus, students will "depart" from four points over a two-semester sequence - and study under four instructors with distinct insights in architectural history.

In the past two years, our instructors have been:

1. Professor Wendy Redfield—presenting topics connected to the work of Peter Zumthor;
2. Professor Ammar Eloueini—presenting topics connected to the work of SAANA (Kazuyo Sejima and Ryau Nishizawa);
3. Professor Ruben Garcia—presenting topics connected to the work of Rafael Moneo;
4. Professor Pankaj Vir Gupta—presenting topics connected to the work of modernist architects in India (including the work of Balkrishna Doshi and Charles Correa)

Curricular Impact

In logistical terms, this change in the structure of our History/Theory sequence has not interrupted the sequence of other courses or studios. We were previously employing four instructors to teach two sequential courses to graduate students and two sequential courses to undergraduates each year. Those arrangements have not changed in our new scenario. However, we believe that the new structure of courses will better enable our students to absorb and contribute in the later Advanced History/Theory seminars they are required to take, and that subsequent work in case studies or precedent analysis will be enhanced by the models of inquiry presented in the new "survey replacement" courses. Further, we believe that the new courses will offer a broader range of voices and vantage-points to explore and interpret the "colorful fish" and to introduce at least four distinct "fishing methodologies."

The *Introduction to Architecture* Course as a Timeline or Framework

The current *Introduction to Architecture* course at the School of Architecture is built around the idea of presenting the major themes, concepts, and practices of architecture through a series of chronologically arranged canonical examples. This course, required for all architecture majors, provides a "framework" or scaffold of architectural vocabulary to support subsequent student courses and help draw the broad outlines of the discipline. As such, this course serves as a rudimentary timeline and canon. There are some 60 or 70 buildings presented from the Parthenon to the Gondo Primary School in Burkina Faso in the Introduction to Architecture course. This material is intended to provide a basic vocabulary and basis for further exploration in subsequent courses. The existing *Introduction to Architecture* course is not intended to substitute for the former survey-style courses but may help to ground the more speculative and idiosyncratic new "survey-replacements" with a degree of consistency and tradition.

Comprehensiveness

Even with the framework presented in the *Introduction to Architecture* course, we recognize that some comprehensiveness and some ancient antecedents will be lost in our new approach. We are willing to sacrifice some detail of the ancient past to allow greater concentration on architectural production since the Enlightenment. We anticipate that there will be some constructive overlap between parts of each pair of seven-week sessions. For instance, some have humorously observed that *"all roads lead to Le Corbusier"* (as well as other figures, buildings, and issues) at some point — and that "coincidence" may be revealing and interesting. Further, we suspect that there will be elements normally covered in conventional survey courses that will not be referenced in any of the new courses — that too will be interesting and revealing and should not be cause for alarm. We are knowingly sacrificing comprehensiveness for diverse and methodical inquiry; and sacrificing some breadth for what we hope will be enriching depth.

Instructors and Diversity of Voices and Subjects
By increasing the number of instructors involved in the sequence, we have more opportunity to introduce diverse points of departure, subject areas, and voices. In our first iterations, these courses have been presented by western, non-western, male, and female instructors; they engage points of departure from two western and two non-western sources; as well as from three male architects and one female architect in the present or very recent past. We believe that this diversity is integral (and potentially fundamental) to each of the courses, rather than simply a gesture or sample of inclusion.

The new system also offers opportunities for many other faculty to participate — and for many other points of departure in the near future. Even in the short time since establishing this shift in delivery, several faculty have expressed interest in creating an offering for the future and several have posed an even more diverse series of points of departure. It may be worth noting that a few of these courses might lend themselves to "Visiting Faculty" members or a similar opportunity. Initial instructors include both PhD faculty and licensed faculty as contributors to these sequences, offering a legible distinction in method as well as focus. This variety and diversity has been welcome and instructive as well.

Kentaro Tsubaki

Favrot Associate Professor of Architecture

The Ethos of Structural Systems Education in the Architecture Curriculum

"Technology is far more than a method. It is a world in itself. As a method it is superior in almost every respect. But only where it is left to itself, as in gigantic structures of engineering, there technology reveals its true nature. There it is evident that it is not only a useful means but that it is something that has a meaning and a powerful form so powerful in fact, that it is not easy to name it. Where technology reaches its real fulfillment it transcends into architecture."

Mies van der Rohe

"It is radical and conservative at once. It is radical in accepting the scientific and technological driving and sustaining forces of our time. It has a scientific character, but it is not science. It uses technological means but it is not technology. It is conservative as it is not only concerned with a purpose but also with a meaning, as it is not only concerned with a function but also with an expression. It is conservative as it is based on the eternal laws of architecture: Order, Space, Proportion."

Mies van der Rohe

Kenneth Frampton unpacks Mies's preoccupation with structure by comparing the above remarks. On one level, it is technical, philosophical, and conservative. It is about a systemic conception from the whole to its constituent parts. He marvels at Mies's remarks as an "evocation of structural rationalism but also for its indirect allusion to medieval scholasticism." [1] On another level, it is about the novelty of structural performance, the radical nature of spatial aesthetics that is afforded to progress in technology and the engineering of the period.

1. Frampton, Kenneth, and John Cava. Studies in Tectonic Culture: The Poetics of Construction in Nineteenth and Twentieth Century Architecture. , 1995. Print. P186.

He then critiques the internal conflict, the "split between the conservative nature of his tectonic structure and radical stance of his spatial aesthetics." Even Mies, who aims to "free the practice of building from the control of the aesthetic speculators," [2] was not immune to secretly or not so secretly harboring the potential of structures manifesting as aesthetical expression.

2. Ibid. P161.

More recently, the U.S. architectural education has been split between mastering the technical competency and theorizing the cultural and aesthetical values. Schools generally differentiate themselves by emphasizing one over the other.

We propose an alternative. We are in the era of Anthropocene. We vow to strategise and adapt to climate change by leveraging the technological performance, the computational power, and the digital network with a complex array of large data sets that it produces. The design process is a negotiation, a judgment on informed tradeoffs amongst diverse sets of competing interests.

Suppose the architectural design is to project, test, and devise the most economical, low-impact three-dimensional distribution of physical materials and assemblies to sustain long-term healthy dwellings. We must be able to systemically and holistically navigate the complex tradeoffs amongst quantifiable performative values (economical, functional, sustainable, etc.) and non-quantifiable personal, aesthetical, and cultural agenda.

The structural systems course at TuSA aims to instill in students the practice of tradeoffs amongst the following values:

Economic Values
1. Buildable floor area and bulk regulation (Zoning)
2. Construction Types (Building Code)
3. Quantity/Weight of the materials and components

Aesthetic/Functional Values
1. Building Massing (Contextual)
2. Floor to Floor and Ceiling Height
3. Occupancy Classification (Program)
4. Column Grid Spacing
5. Lateral Bracing Location

Structural Performative Values
1. Typical Structural Bay Size and Tributary Area
2. Spread Footing Size
3. Lateral Bracing Size
4. Beam/Girder/Column Connection Size
5. Horizontal Member Structural Depth and Weight
6. Column Size and Weight

Fig. 3, 4 (Right, Below)

Images from "Analytical Design of Steel Frame Structure," final project by Jose Varela (Fall 2021).

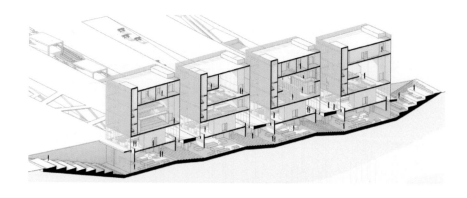

= 44.05

Top Floor y-y axis

K = .75

Slenderness Ratio: k x L/r = .75 x 152.0" / .81"

= 140.74 y-y governs

Fcrit: $\pi^2 E/Sr^2$

= π^2 x 30000ksi/ 140.74 in^2 = 14.94

= 14.9ksi < 30 ksi

Column will buckle before crushing

Pcrit: Fcrit x A

= 14.9ksi x 4.41in^2 = 65.7

=65.7k < 688.26k

Column overloaded

Ground Floor x-x axis:

K=1

L = (20' x12") – 18" = 222"

Slenderness Ratio: k x L/r = 1 x 222" / 3.95"

= 56.2

Ground Floor y-y axis:

K= .75

L = (20' x 12") – 40 = 200

Slenderness Ratio: k x L/r = .75 x 200 / .81

= 185.185 y-y governs

Fcrit: $\pi^2 E/Sr^2$

= π^2 x 30000ksi/ 180.2in^2 = 8.62ksi

Pcrit: Fcrit x A

8.62k x 4.41in^2 = 38.01k < 688.26k

Column Overloaded

Required Moment of Inertia

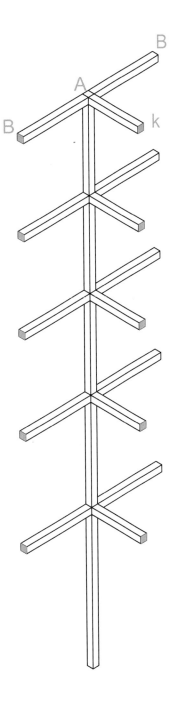

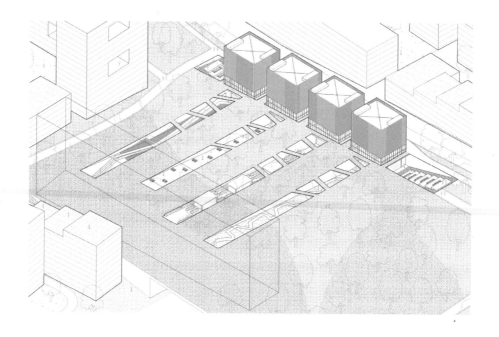

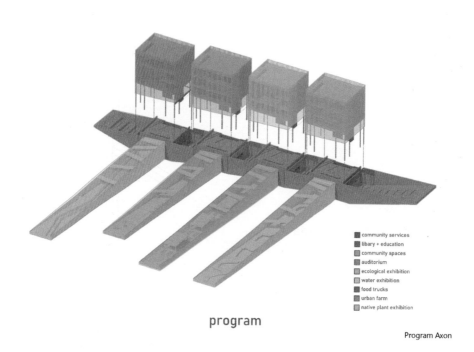

- community services
- libary + education
- community spaces
- auditorium
- ecological exhibition
- water exhibition
- food trucks
- urban farm
- native plant exhibition

program

Program Axon

The methodology to calculate the performative values is based on the fundamentals of physics. It is introduced systematically and carefully contextualized against economic, aesthetic, and functional concerns. The final project asks students to synthesize the gained knowledge by comprehensively designing a steel frame structure appropriate for a past studio project of their choice. Students are confronted with the tradeoffs between the various values negotiating the design intent and physical constraints for the first time.

The Structural Systems course emphasizes the relationships between parameters of structural framing systems and their impact on design decisions. It instills a basic set of vocabulary necessary for future architects to lead the engineers and contractors confidently. However, the ultimate motive of the course is to elucidate and conscientiously position students' hidden architectural values and agenda within the normative architectural practice as we tackle ever-more complex problems in a rapidly changing world.

Fig. 5, 6 (Left, Below)

Images from "Analytical Design of Steel Frame Structure," final project by Jose Varela (Fall 2021).

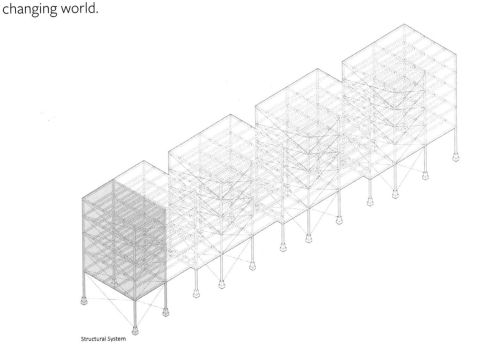

Structural System

DIGITAL MEDIA

Norman [C]

Digital Media I introduces digital tools and techniques for their application in architectural production. The primary objective is the cultivation of a drawing practice that facilitates critical thinking, the testing of design ideas, and effective communication. Each week explores fundamental concepts in architectural representation that include a range of two- and three-dimensional media and workflows.

Students work through orthographic (plan, section, elevation), axonometric, and perspective projection drawings of mixed media with an overall emphasis of the integration of digital drawing techniques.

The course uses lecture and workshop formats to foster critical perspectives and technique development, respectively. Classes consist of lectures, discussions, workshops, and pin-up critiques. Lectures situate the content in historical and professional domains and articulate lesson objectives. In addition, the workshop format is meant to aid content development and assist with questions regarding the week's assignment by working through lesson goals collectively. Upon successful completion of the course, students are proficient in skills and concepts underlying the representational strategies to produce architecture.

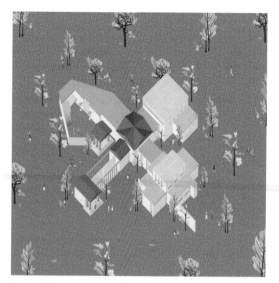

Anna Kathryn Becker

Jose Varela

Vivien Hartin

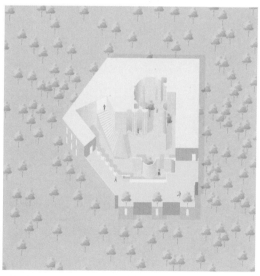

Chelsa Kilgore

s> Elizabeth Keigler   **i>** Carrie Norman

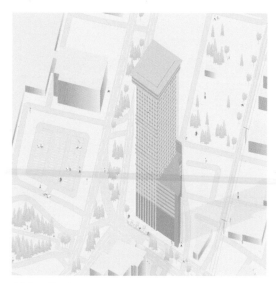

Abby Carlton

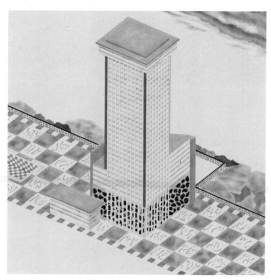

Anna Kathryn Becker

Amanda Bond

James Poche

Georgia Clarke

Jake Davis

Olivia Vercruysse

Miya Kutchins

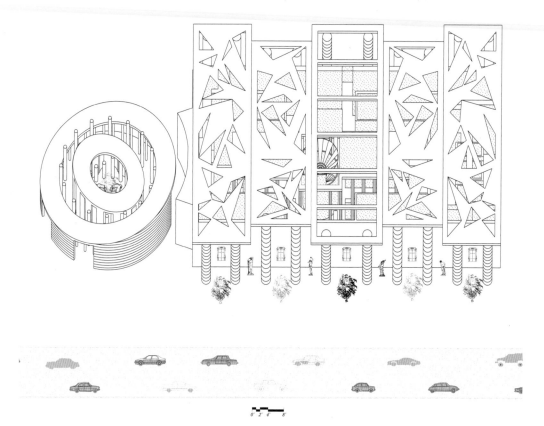

s> Yazmine Parker

s> Bradley Hyatt

i> Carrie Norman

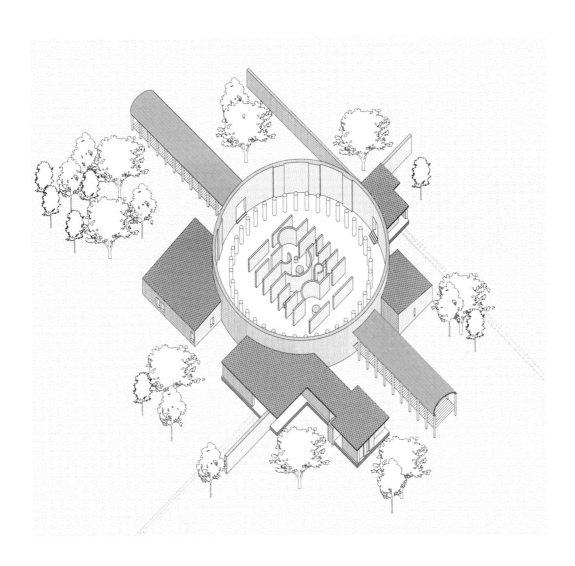

ADVANCED DIGITAL MEDIA

Modesitt [C]

The Digital Media course sequence introduces students to the principles, conventions, and modes of architectural representation. The sequence is intended to (1) develop proficiency in digital techniques underpinning contemporary architectural practice and discourse, and (2) establish a critical framework for understanding representational techniques as historical and conceptual instruments. The primary objective of the sequence is to cultivate digital practices that facilitate critical thinking, iterative testing of design ideas, and effective communication. Both courses in the sequence are composed of a combination of lectures, discussions, labs, and pin-up critiques.

Advanced Digital Media is the second course of the sequence and covers advanced techniques for digital image production. As a gateway to advanced digital media, this course begins with two software platforms, 3ds Max 2020 (Autodesk) and V-Ray Next (Chaos Group). Each of these software packages are robust, powerful platforms with a wide range of functionality. These two software packages are the professional standard for architectural visualization, used by small and big offices alike. They are also gateways for exploring visualization for other disciplines, professions, and industries. In addition to image production, they include a diverse range of functionality that incorporates concepts such as parametric modeling, UI "tree" structures, physical simulations, animation, and BIM (building information modeling).

s> Samantha Staviss
s> Alex DiSimone

i> Adam Modesitt

s> Seth Laskin
s> Delaney Smith

i> Adam Modesitt

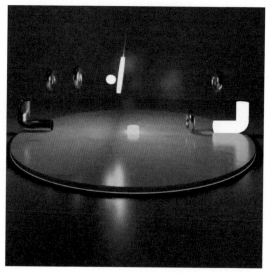

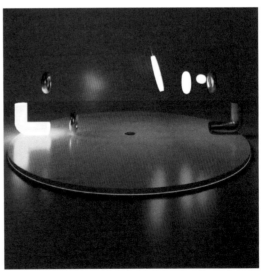

s> Clara Gardner

s> Lebryant Bell

i> Adam Modesitt

what for

what for

research studios

RESILIENCE REINFORCED

Instructed by Kentaro Tsubaki

This studio focused on the role of the landscape in architectural design and the development of basic skills in site analysis, site design, and site representation. Site characteristics were understood as both natural (a result of the actions of nature) and cultural (a result of the actions of people).

Students were introduced to a range of conceptual strategies for articulating the relationship between building and site, and developed the ability to sculpt the surface of the land to accommodate human activities.

The course highlighted the designer's ethical obligations to the larger network of social and ecological systems and conditions. Building design themes included spatial organization and hierarchy, circulation, structure, and enclosure. The studio was integrated with digital media classes to ensure that students gained fluency in computer-aided design processes, drawing, spatial modeling, and digital design techniques.

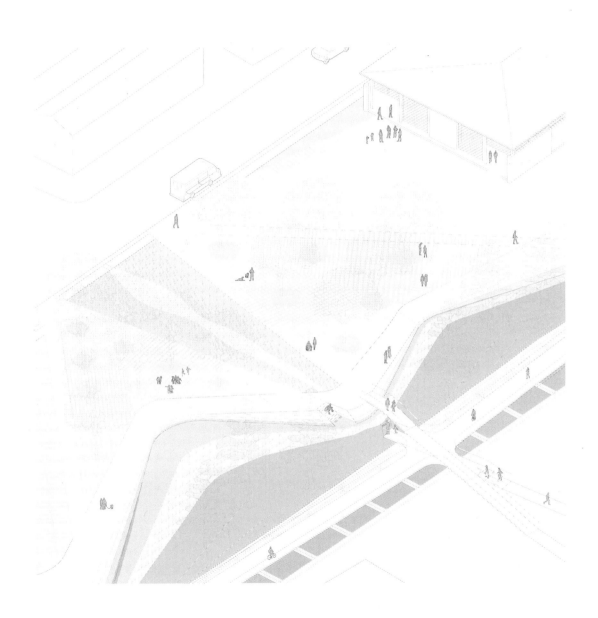

s> Gabrielle Rashleigh   i> Kentaro Tsubaki

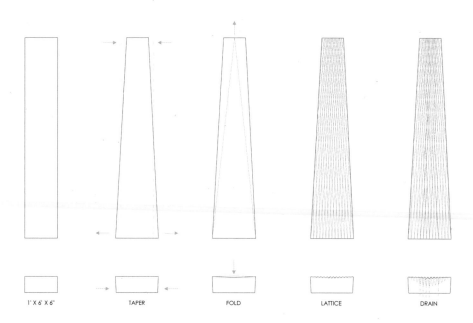

1' X 6' X 6"   TAPER   FOLD   LATTICE   DRAIN

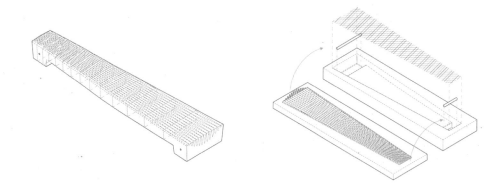

s> Gabrielle Rashleigh   **i>** Kentaro Tsubaki

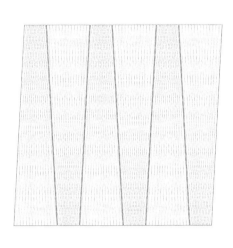

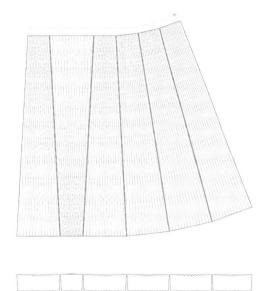

BRIDGE

TURN

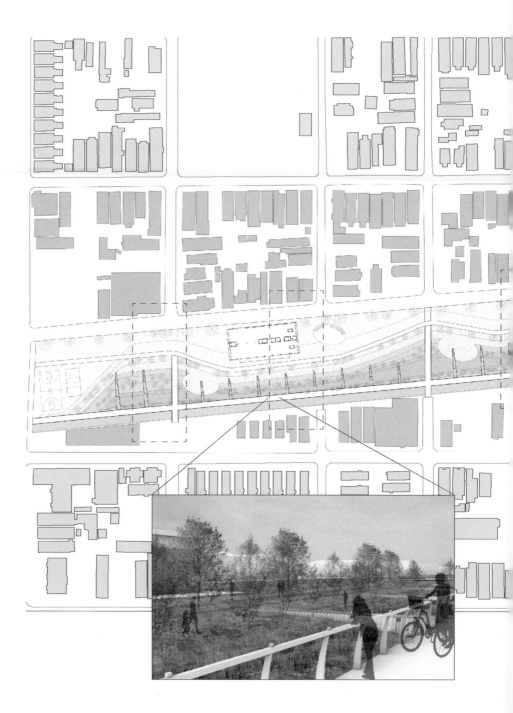

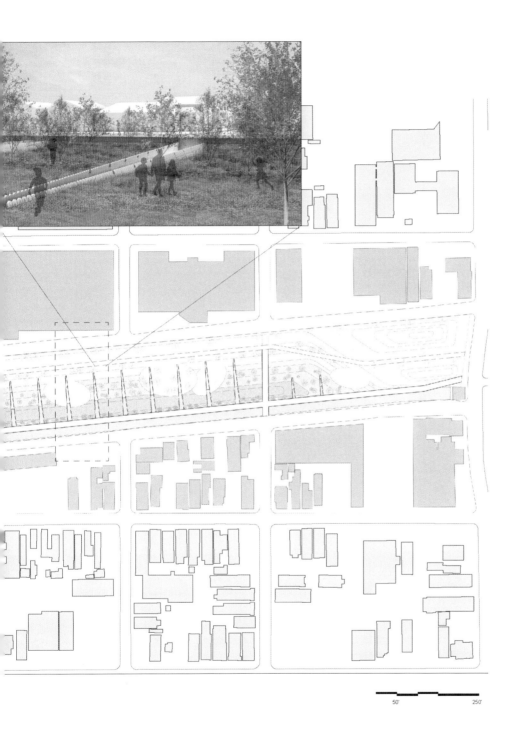

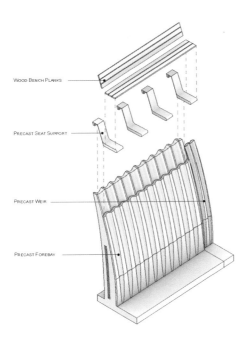

WOOD BENCH PLANKS

PRECAST SEAT SUPPORT

PRECAST WEIR

PRECAST FOREBAY

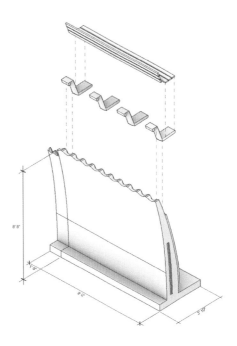

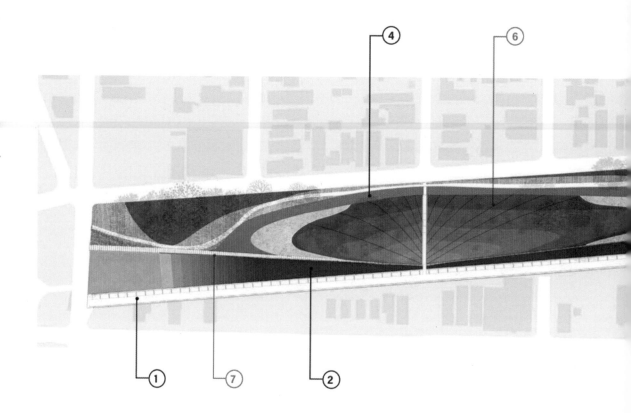

PRIMARY WATER
MANAGEMENT

(1) ST. LOUIS CANAL

(2) FOREBAY (162,135 CUBIC FEET)

(3) OCCUPYABLE DETENTION BASIN (382,734.4 CUBIC FEET)

(4) BIOSWALE (79,399051 CUBIC FEET)

(5) FORESTED MARSH (APPROXIMATELY 33,367 CUBIC FEET)

TOTAL WATER RETAINED ON SITE= APPROX. 657, 636.18 CUBIC FEET

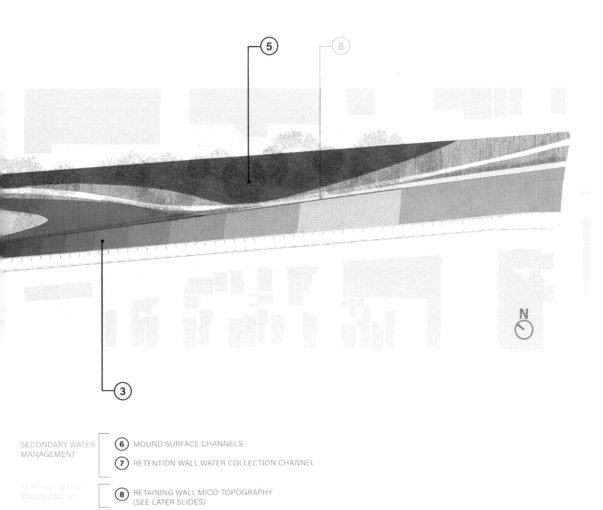

SECONDARY WATER
MANAGEMENT

⑥ MOUND SURFACE CHANNELS

⑦ RETENTION WALL WATER COLLECTION CHANNEL

TERTIARY WATER
MANAGEMENT

⑧ RETAINING WALL MICO-TOPOGRAPHY
(SEE LATER SLIDES)

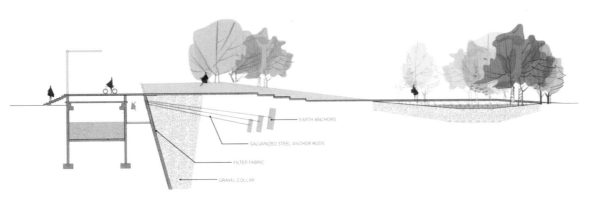

EARTH ANCHORS

GALVANIZED STEEL ANCHOR RODS

FILTER FABRIC

GRAVEL COLLAR

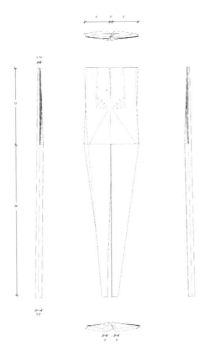

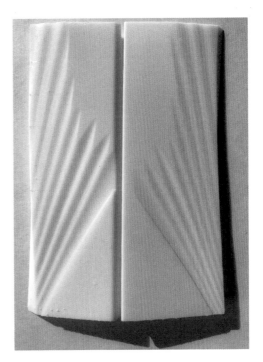

THE FUTURE OF PORTS

Instructed by Margarita Jover

In New Orleans, the Inner Harbor Navigation Canal (inside yellow line at the image above) constitutes a large industrial and economic infrastructure for the city of New Orleans and the surrounding region. Today these five miles of waterfront property, in close proximity to key low-density residential neighborhoods and the city center, are in a state of economic decay, poor ecology, and disarticulated urbanity. Guided by a multidisciplinary team of faculty, students at Tulane School of Architecture will document these properties and buildings, research comparable examples and best practices worldwide, and propose innovative Design-Research projects to engage stakeholders and citizens at large about how best to utilize and sustain the property over the next 50 years.

The ultimate goal of this Research Studio was to drive university knowledge towards the public sphere and to reinforce the debate about the future of the city of New Orleans — our commons — in a political moment in which many decisions about the future of cities are made in private global spheres. The role of Design-Research on this type of large-scale urban transformations is key for two main reasons: one is educational, and the other is political. The educational motivation was to teach students and the public that architecture is a holistic discipline, able to formalize and visualize large-scale transformations and long-term urban scenarios to seek urban equity, improved ecology, and sustainable economy.

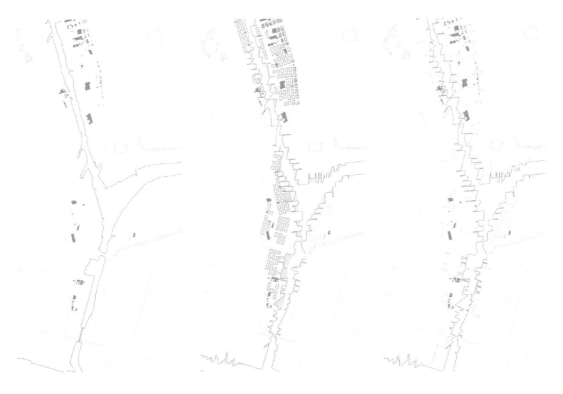

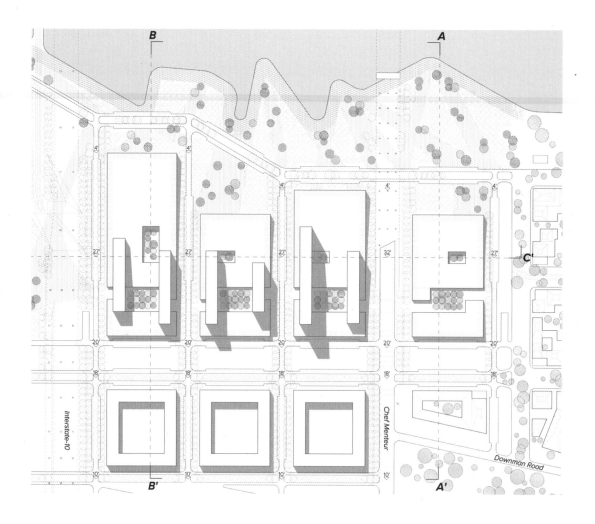

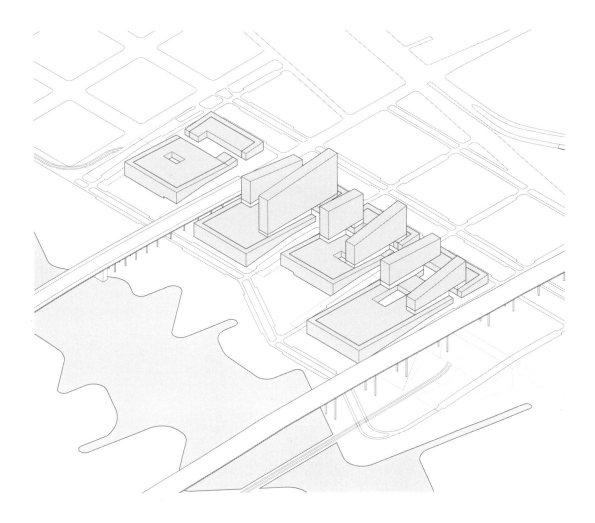

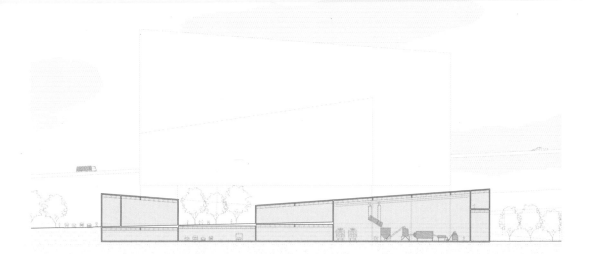

s> Jonathan Michka   i> Margarita Jover

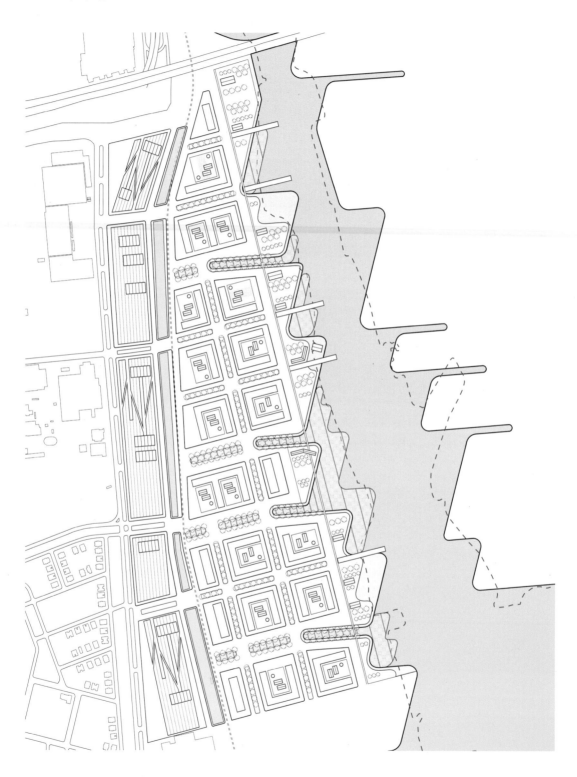

s> Annie Davis   **i>** Margarita Jover

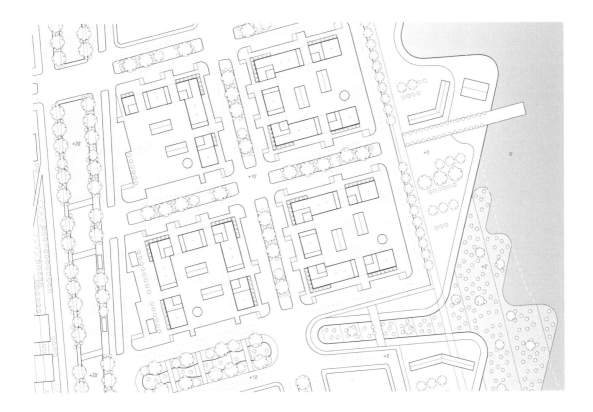

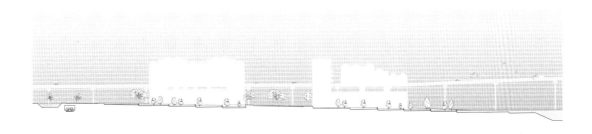

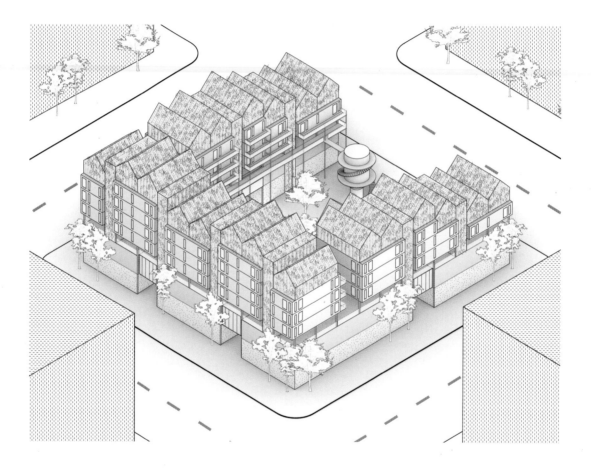

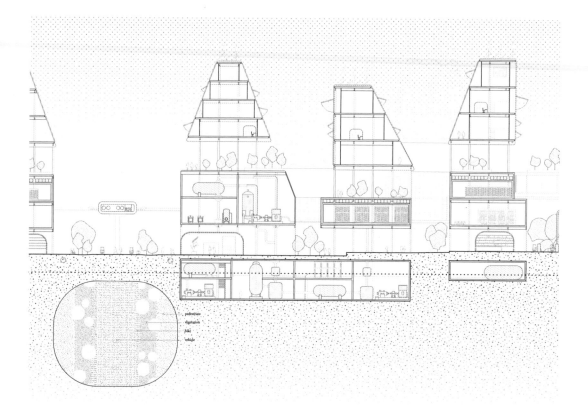

OFFCUTS & CASTOFFS

Instructed by Adam Modesitt

Industrialization mechanized building material processing and ushered in the modern era of material standardization. Standardization is now so universal, it is difficult to imagine architecture without it. The appeal is easy to understand. Standardization simplifies distribution and construction, offering predictability and interchangeability.

Yet the benefits of standardization belie a devil's bargain. The privileging of standardization above all else has created material supply chains that define efficiency only in the most narrow of terms. The blinkered focus on standardization excludes building materials that manifest irregularity, disregards native material strengths, and neglects total embodied energy costs. Despite increasingly elaborate manufacturing processes, standardization is often grossly inefficient when considered in the context of entire material lifecycles.

Offcuts & Castoffs casts a critical eye towards the tradeoffs inherent to standardization. The studio will explore alternative material futures, though work will be grounded in the present reality of standardized material supply chains and construction practices. Offcuts & Castoffs will begin by looking at waste in the margins, at materials and methods that fall just outside the purview of standardization.

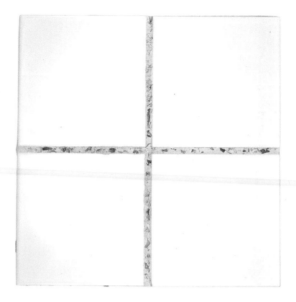

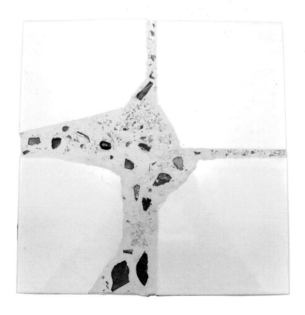

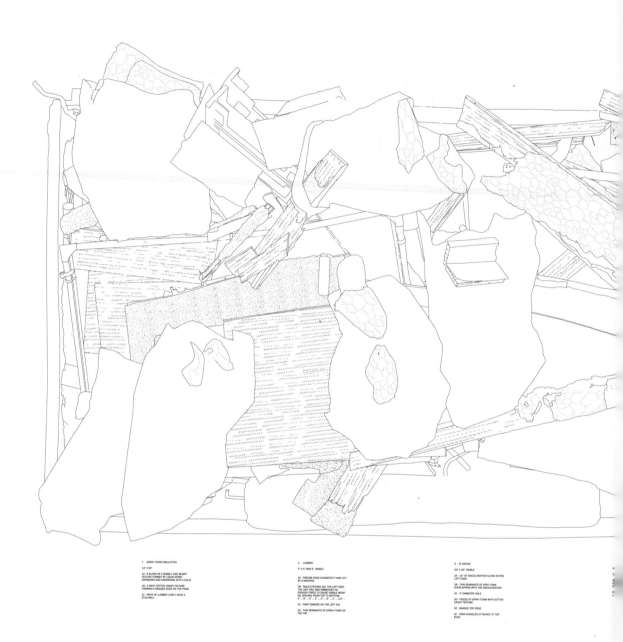

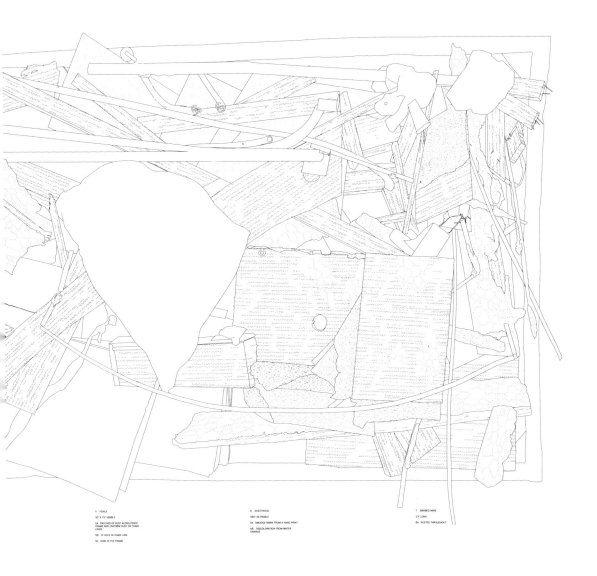

5   FENCE

30" X 75" VISIBLE

5A   PATCHES OF RUST ALONG FENCE
FRAME AND UNIFORM RUST ON CHAIN
LINKS

5B   9" HOLE IN CHAIN LINK

5C   KINK IN THE FRAME

6   SHEETROCK

485" 5A VISIBLE

6A   SMUDGE MARK FROM A HAND PRINT

6B   DISCOLORATION FROM WATER
DAMAGE

7   BARBED WIRE

13' LONG

6A   RUSTED THROUGHOUT

SMALL CENTER BUILD_ Apothecarts

Instructed by Emilie Taylor-Welty and Nick Jenisch

This studio aimed to create innovative designers who understand the basics of building and who know how to engage, collaborate, and execute projects with a public interest. This studio, which was supported and based out of the Albert and Tina Small Center for Collaborative Design, designed and fabricated a project with a partner organization in the New Orleans community. Working closely with stakeholders throughout the semester, students responded to the cultural, environmental, and material challenges presented. The outcome of the fall semester was work built in collaboration with peers, consisting of a balance between individually designed work and group design development.

This studio partnered with Prisoner's Apothecary, a local organization that makes tinctures and plant medicine for communities most deeply impacted by the insidious reach of mass incarceration. The design team was asked to design and fabricate mobile healing units that expanded the reach of the project and created new opportunities for conversation and education around mass incarceration. Through research and prototyping, students designed a series of bike-powered apothecary carts that can be deployed across New Orleans.

Students: Adrian Evans, Jeremy Boudy, Lizzie Bateman, Anna Deeg, Rebecca Dunn, Bhumika Shirole, Claire DiVito, Zach Speroni, Dana Ridenour, Danielle Martin, Daniella Scheeringa, James Rennert

Partners: jackie summell from Solitary Gardens; Jen Stovall and students from the Samara School of Community Herbalism; Resurrection after Exoneration

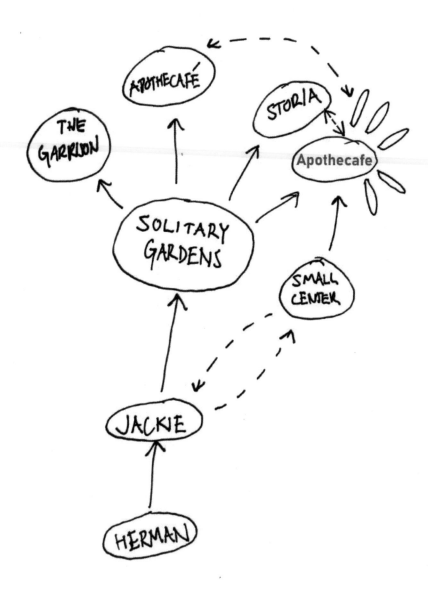

Storage   Materials   Transportation

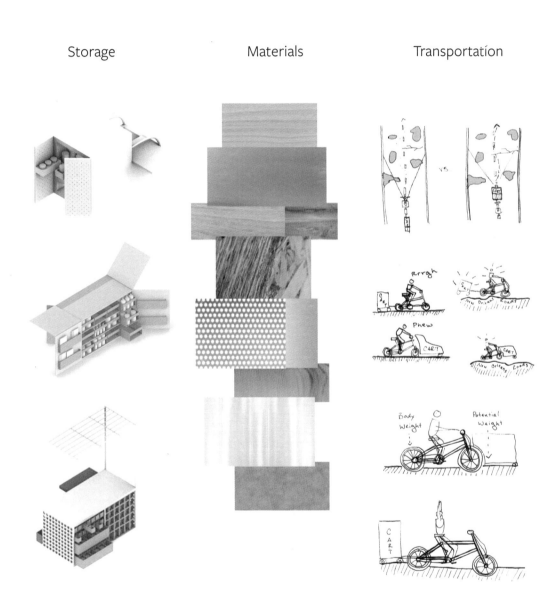

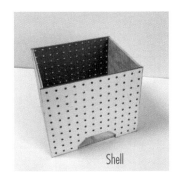
Shell

Handeled insert

Nested

Glass jar holder

Sample jar

Jar holder attaches to exterior

Spill proof bottom

Tall handle

Larger wire mesh

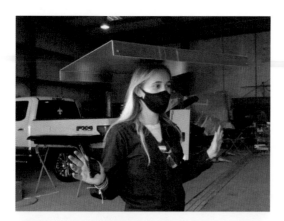

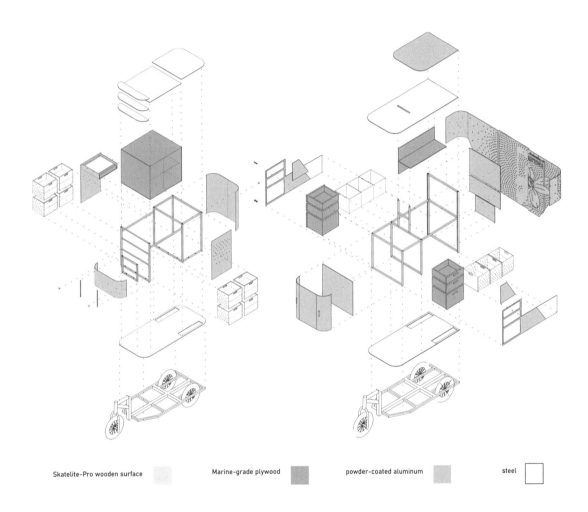

Skatelite-Pro wooden surface   Marine-grade plywood   powder-coated aluminum   steel

Camelback

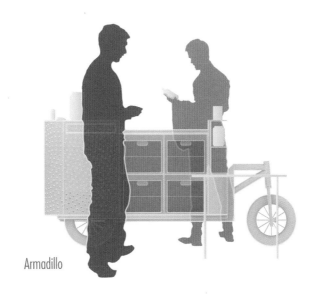

Armadillo

CONTEMPORARY ARCHITECTURE IN HISTORIC CONTEXTS

Instructed by Ammar Eloueini

Architecture is a political act that has social and cultural implications.

This research studio focused on contemporary architectural interventions in historic contexts. New Orleans is the oldest, most preserved city in the United States. It is the perfect laboratory to investigate and test possible contemporary architectural interventions. For its second year, the studio focused on the stretch of Magazine Street between Calliope Street and Jackson Avenue. In recent years, this area has undergone construction and seen some contemporary development take place, creating a "light industrial" vibe. Students studied the historic fabric and the new developments, working on a number of new proposals aimed at densifying the built environment using mixed-use developments.

The specificity of a place is constant, whereas the identity gradually evolves. It is important for architects to be aware and deliberate when making decisions of this distinction, as participants are actors in the evolution of the identity of a place.

s> Bruno Soria Tarazano, Aaron LaGraize   i> Ammar Eloueini

ADDIS ABABA RIVER CITY

Instructed by Ruben Garcia Rubio

The Addis Ababa River City Research Project was created to address challenges in climate change and rapid urbanization in Ethipia through design. The main objective of this research project was to design a holistic urban resilience and regenerative strategy for Addis Ababa, where its main elements are the more than 50 kilometers of river tributaries that weave through the city. Essentially, this project proposes to give back the leading role to the water. The project proposes a new "ecological infrastructure" that uses the river as the main element to tackle the most urgent challenges of the city and, given the morphology of the city, to reach most parts of the population.

The methodology of the project was organized into three different scales. The first one analyzed the development of the city in terms of history, ecology, economics, and culture. The second scale proposed solutions to the issues found in the analysis through a comprehensive master plan, in this case, for a specific area: Upper Kebena River watershed. This "ecological infrastructure" is composed of several layers: restoration of the basin to create a linear park, creation of water parks for a new water and waste management system, encouragement of new public facilities, and the proposal of a slow mobility system. Finally, the third and smallest scale included specific architectural interventions at the most urgent and significant sites highlighted by the master plan.

This studio was the second iteration of a long-term and inter-disciplinary research program led by the Tulane School of Architecture.

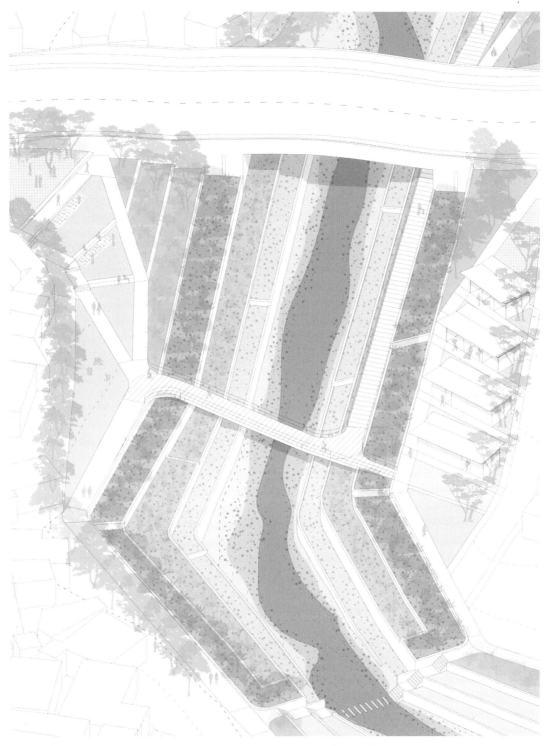

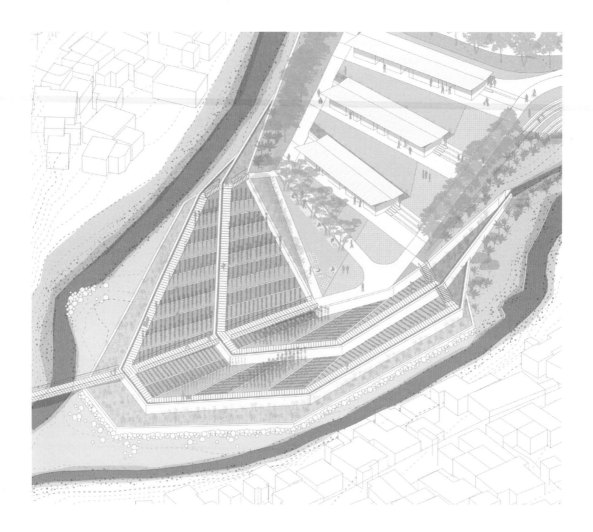

s> Kareem Elsandouby   i> Ruben Garcia Rubio

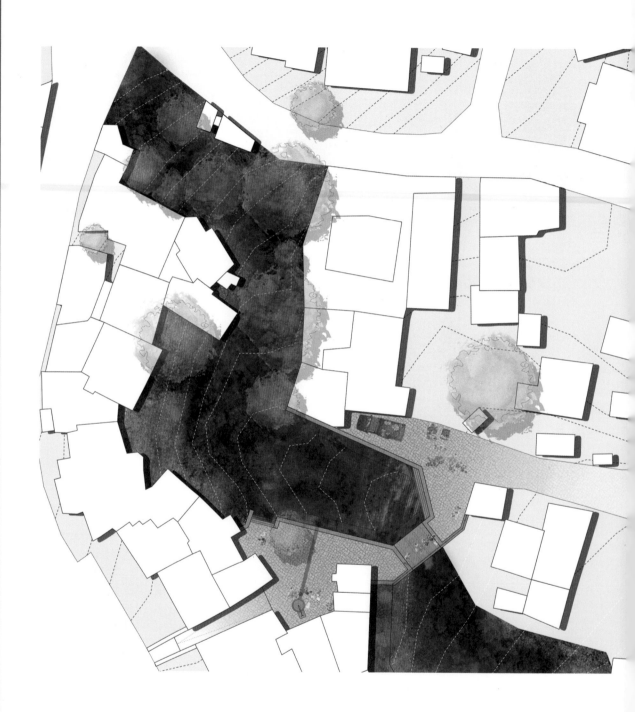

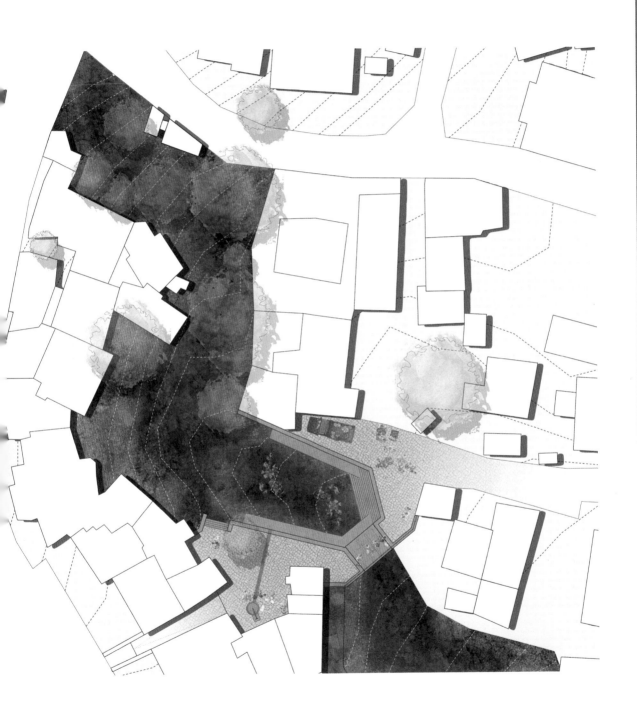

YAMUNA RIVER PROJECT

Instructed by Iñaki Alday, Pankaj Vir Gupta, and Monisha Nasa

The Yamuna River Project is a long-term, interdisciplinary research program with the objective to revitalize the ecology of the Yamuna River in Delhi, India. This studio was the seventh edition of this research studio and the first of a new phase commencing at Tulane University. Led by Dean Iñaki Alday, Pankaj Vir Gupta, and Monisha Nasa, this studio focused on revitalizing the Yamuna River and recovering its connections to Delhi's urban fabric by developing a comprehensive vision and strategic interventions.

The studio was conceived as a research team that combines collective and individual work, with the expectation of three outcomes:

1. An individual urban project, most likely a building, integrated in the urban context. The decision of site, program, and area of intervention will emerge from the study and deliberate proposal of urban strategy.

2. A collective Master Plan, developed by the studio as a team, that will build upon work from the previous phase.

3. A substantial body of research, with graphic synthesis, on the different urban layers that create the city: socio-economics, ecologies, infrastructures, mobility, culture, physical urban fabric, etc.

Over the longer term, the Yamuna River Project's objective is to build a publicly accessible body of knowledge and expertise that will catalyze efforts to reinvigorate the Yamuna's ecological system in Delhi.

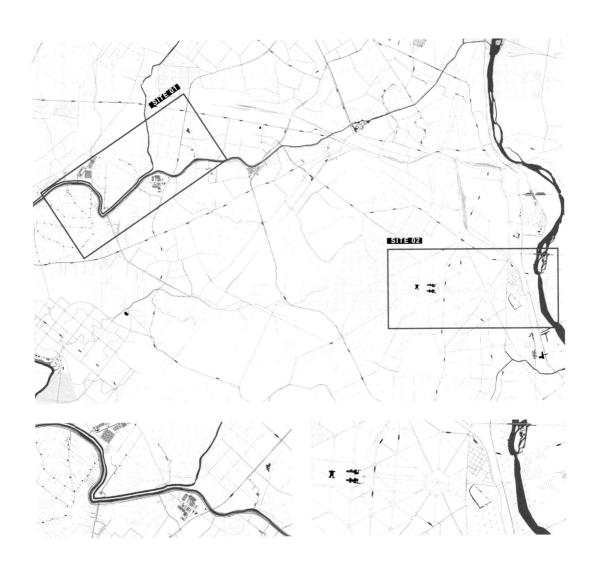

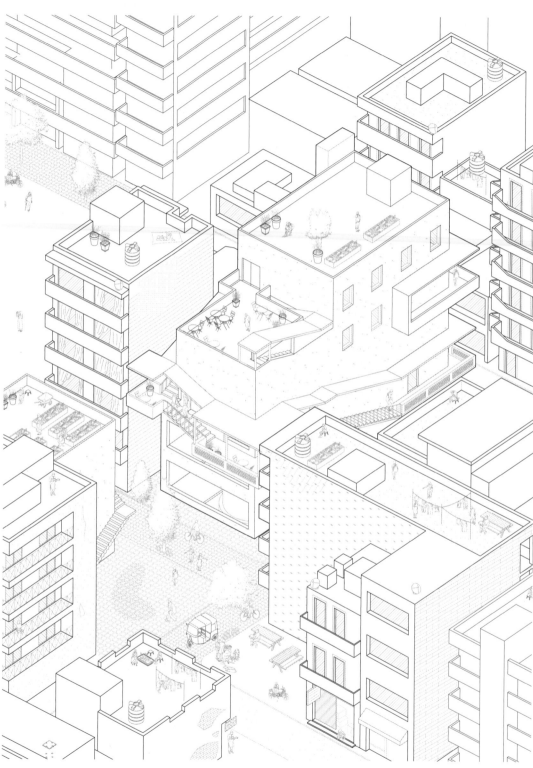

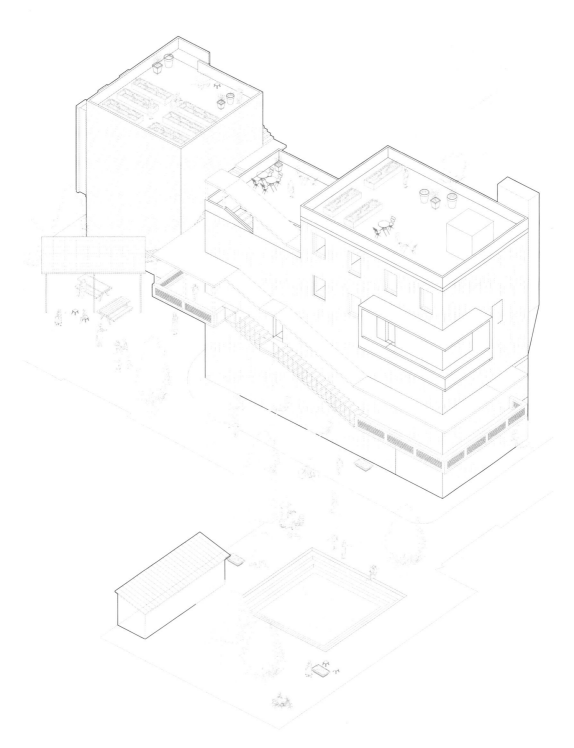

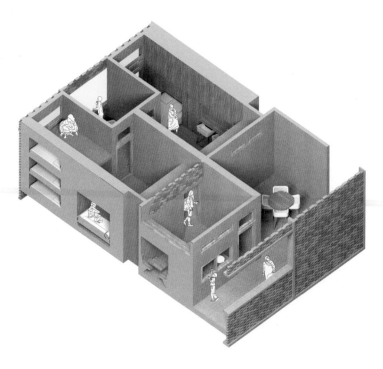

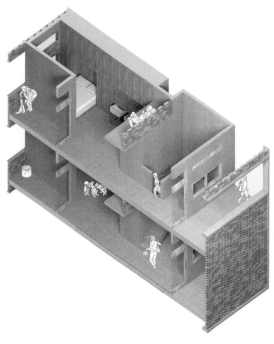

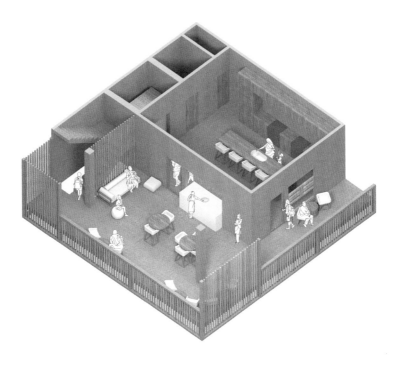

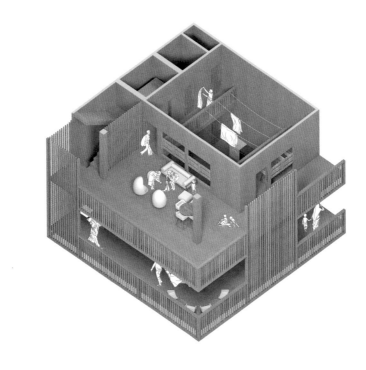

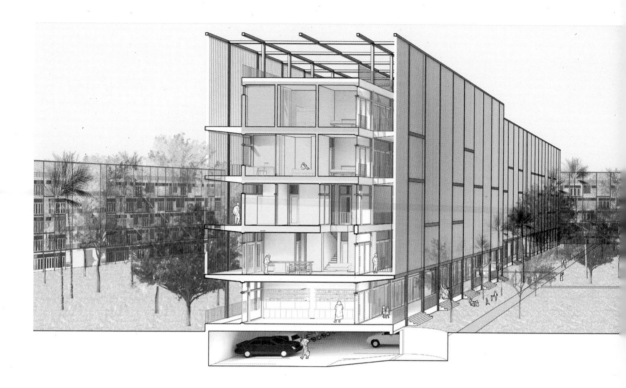

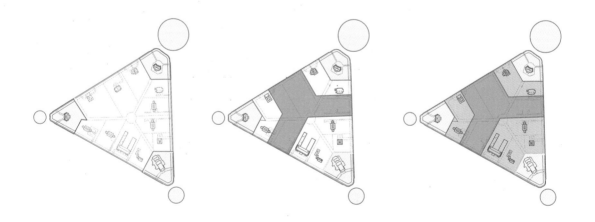

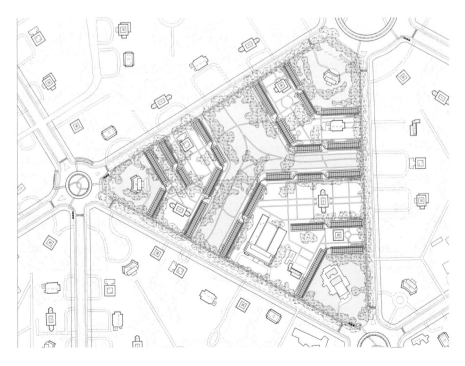

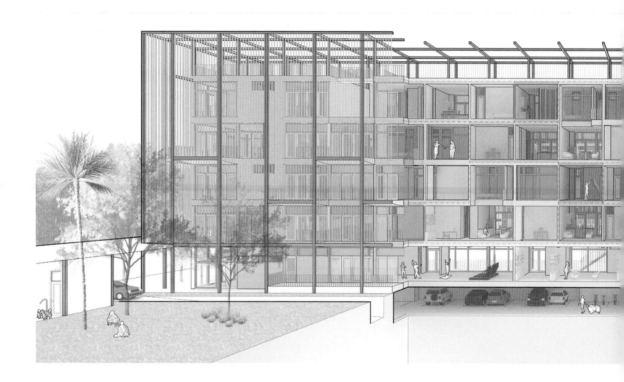

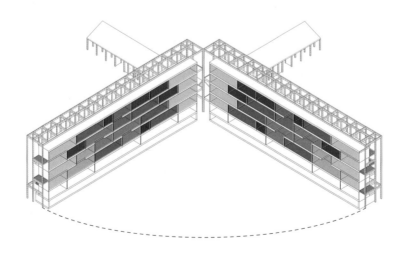

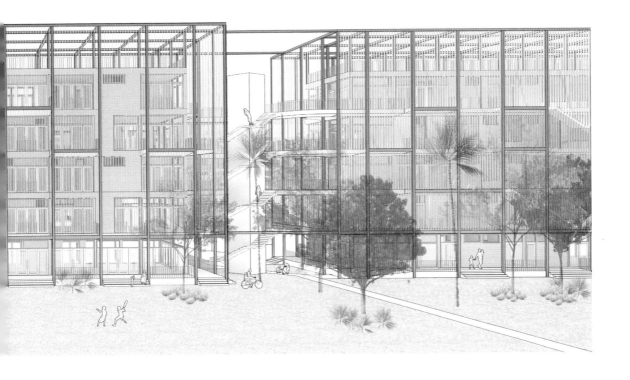

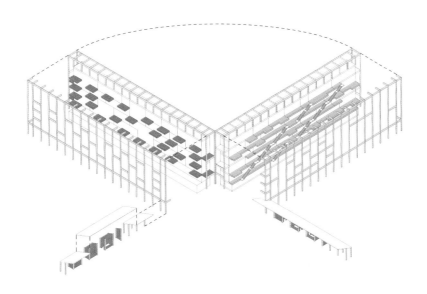

MASS TIMBER AND POST-PANDEMIC DWELLING

Instructed by Judith Kinnard and Rafael Novais Passarelli

Mass timber has potential to support well-being and health in urban dwellings while sequestering carbon and supporting regional rural economies. In the post-pandemic context, these themes should expand to include prototypes for residential construction that challenge standard developer typologies and normative construction methods. These themes were explored in a research studio that considered metrics of material efficiency, global warming potential, and public health. Projects considered air quality and ventilation in high density living, material lifecycle, and design for disassembly.

This upper-level research studio is part of a multi-year investigation in the role of mass timber in building resilience in urban and rural areas in forestry regions. Lecturers from the academic and professional communities contributed to the studio by providing critical perspectives on forestry, timber structural properties, building biome, and biophilic themes. Student projects combined design visualization of the microbial "unseen," with normative explorations of form and performance metrics.

s> Malina Pickard, Kelsie Donovan, Katie Schultz

i> Judith Kinnard, Rafael Passarelli

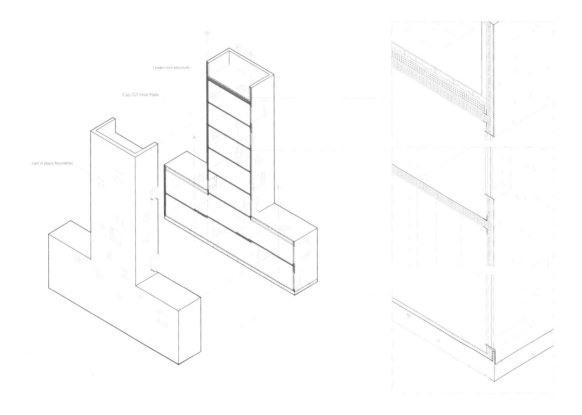

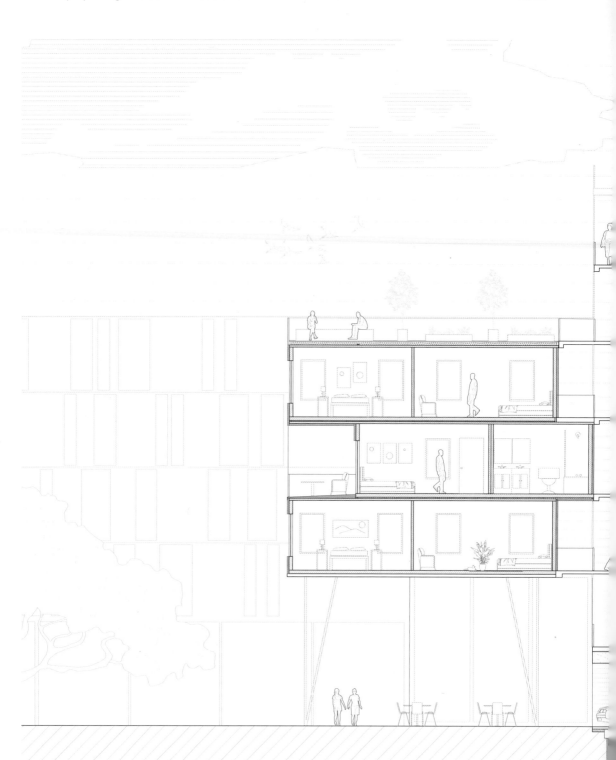

s> Malina Pickard, Kelsie Donovan, Katie Schultz

i> Judith Kinnard, Rafael Passarelli

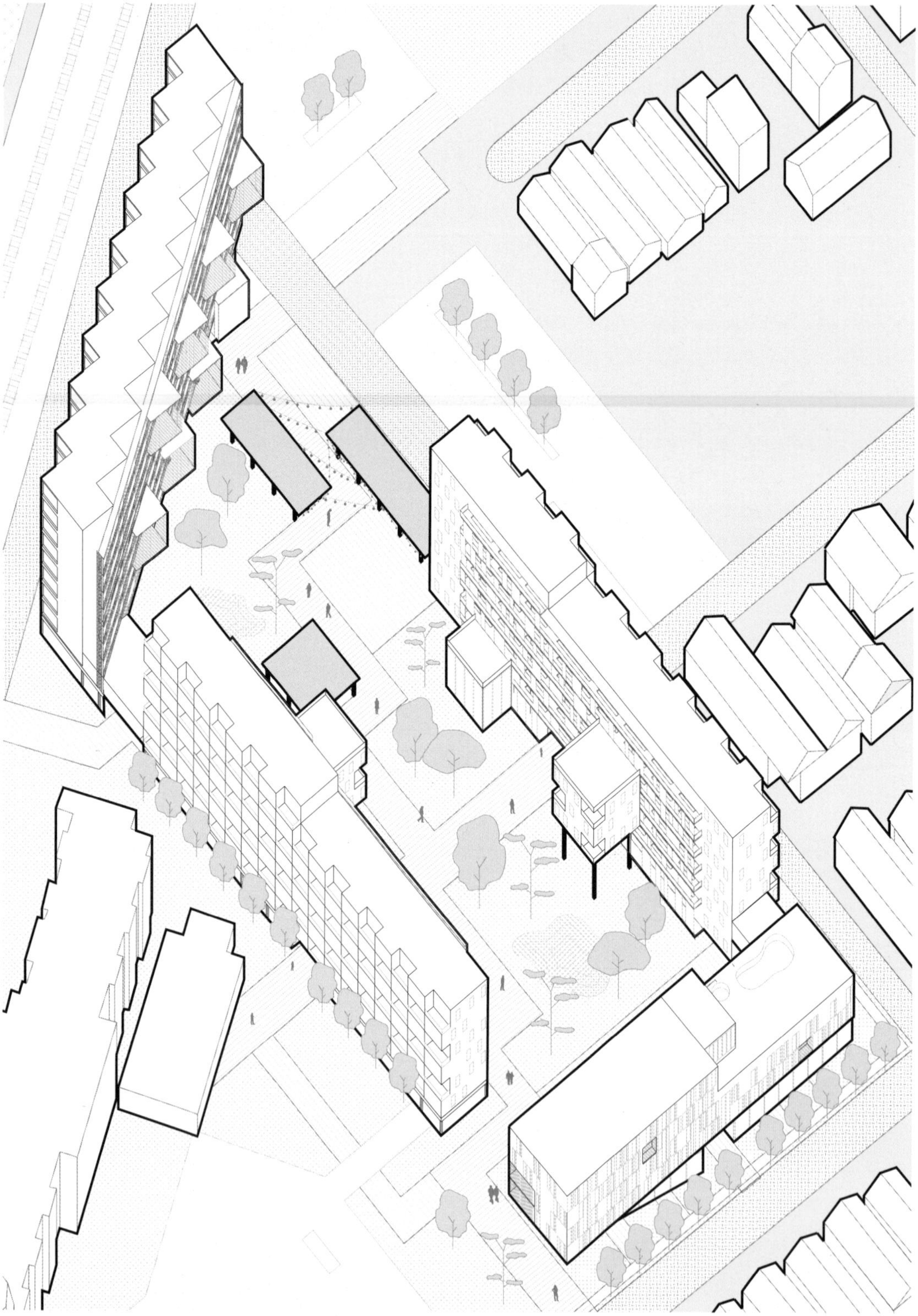

s> Malina Pickard, Kelsie Donovan, Katie Schultz

i> Judith Kinnard, Rafael Passarelli

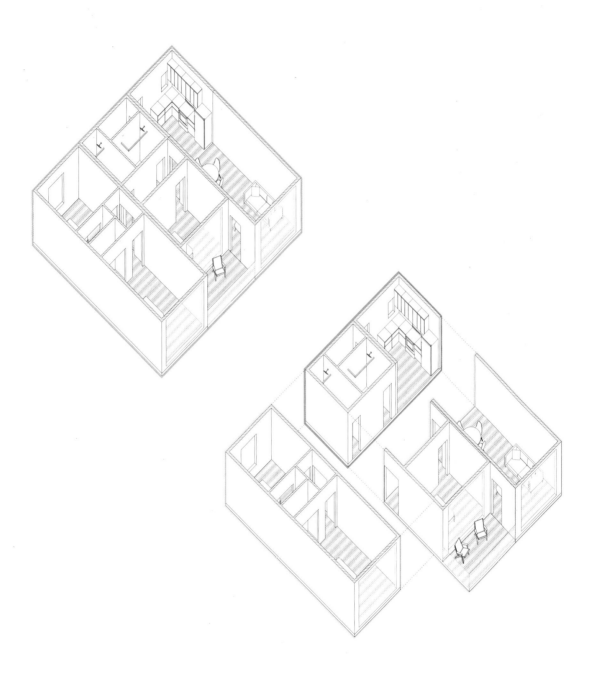

s> Malina Pickard, Kelsie Donovan, Katie Schultz

i> Judith Kinnard, Rafael Passarelli

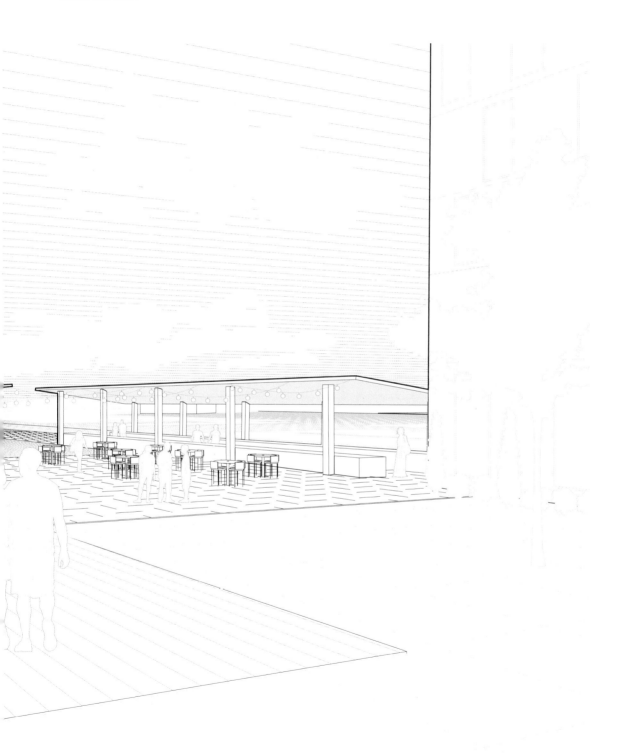

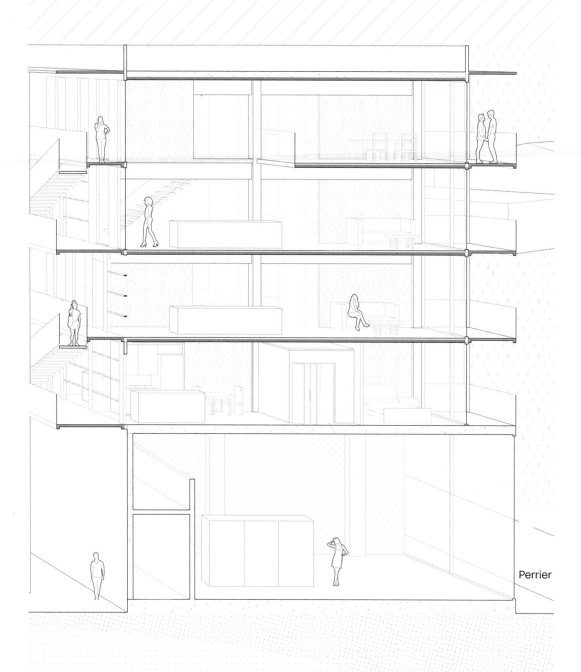

Perrier

s> Natalie Rendleman, Valentina Mancera, Jonathan Michka   **i>** Judith Kinnard, Rafael Passarelli

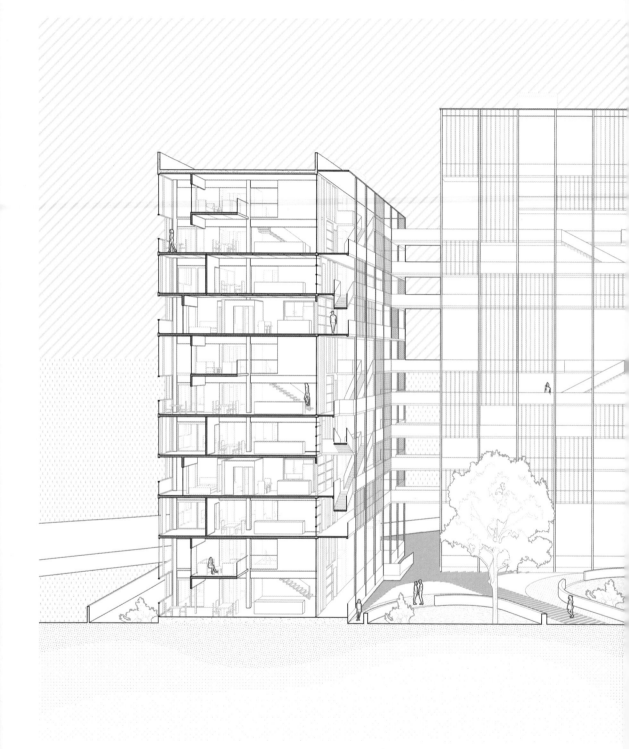

s> Natalie Rendleman, Valentina Mancera,   i> Judith Kinnard, Rafael Passarelli
Jonathan Michka

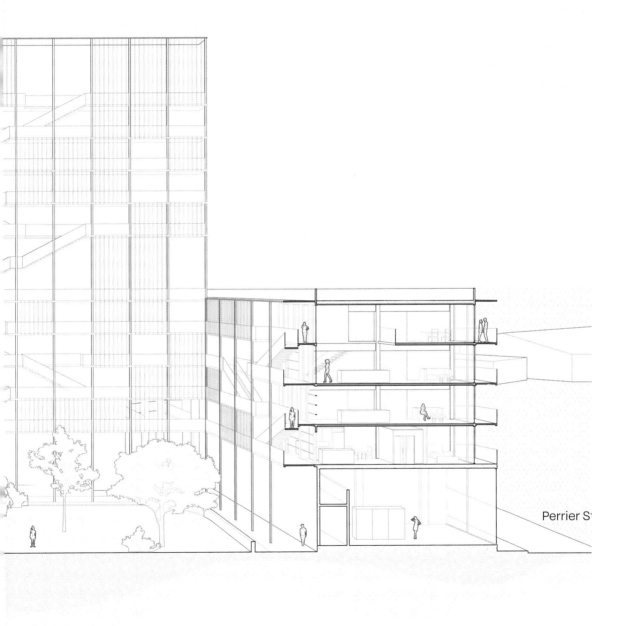

Perrier S

URBANBUILD 16

Instructed by Byron Mouton

URBANBuild 16, a year-long studio, developed and fabricated a dwelling prototype sited in the Central City neighborhood of New Orleans. Neighborhood Housing Services of New Orleans (NHS) committed to providing a site for the project: 2721 Baronne Street.

Debate continues with regard to what should be done with the many historically marginalized areas of largely low-income, underprivileged communities of this city. During the fall semester, several housing strategies were developed in response to and in support of the physical and cultural priorities of the common residential site. One was selected for construction.

The spring studio group worked at the scale of dwelling and fabrication, focusing on material issues and the development of fabrication details through the realization of a built project. Fifteen substantial projects have already been designed and constructed by the School's URBANbuild program, and students continued to build upon the lessons offered by those accomplishments.

Students: Zachary Braaten, Hayley Burroughs, Cheryl Chen, Joanne Engelhard, Hugh Jackson, Erik Luthringshausen, Taylor Naftali, Alec Paulson, David Rodriguez, Trey Sarter, Walid Shahin, Harrison Sturner

Professor: Byron Mouton
Research Assistant: Rafael Passarelli
Partners: New Orleans Neighborhood Housing Services; Nicole Mehaffey, Gould Evans

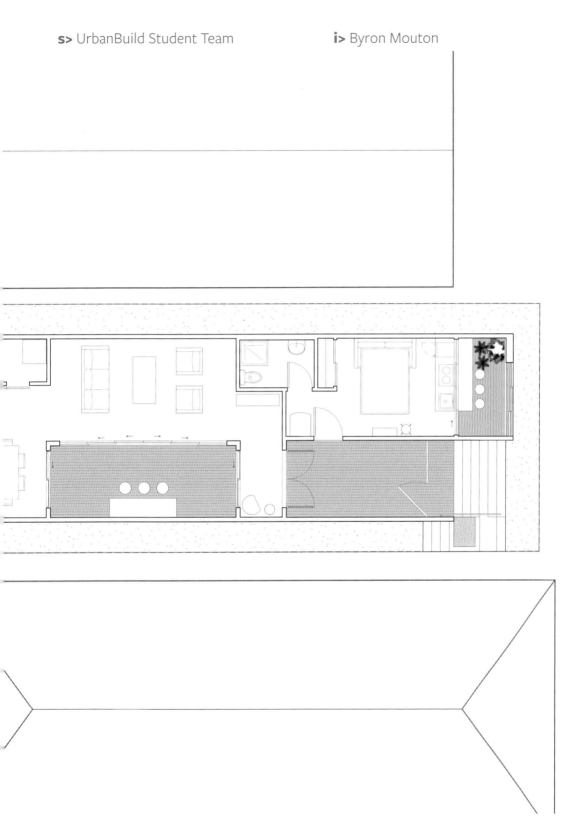

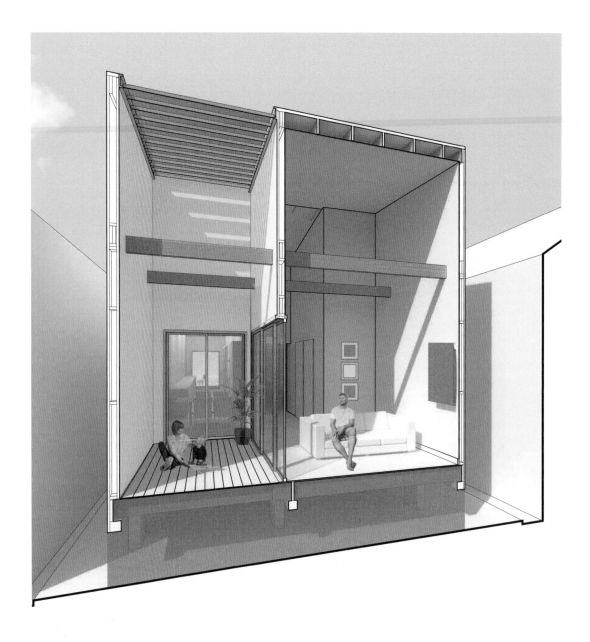

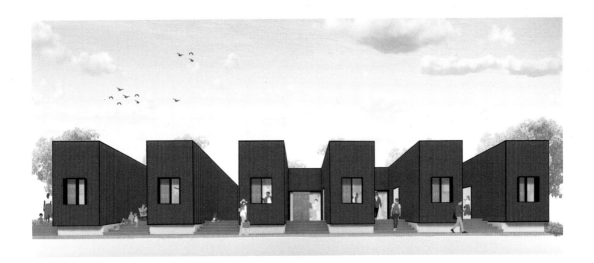

1

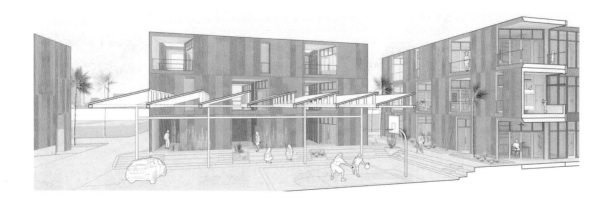

what for

final thesis

FINAL THESIS
A DEVELOPING FRAMEWORK

Author: Jorge Blandin, Joanne Engelhard
Advisors: Ammar Eloueini, Cordula Roser Gray

Haiti Post 2010 Earthquake Living

The 2010 earthquake damaged and destroyed 295,000 homes displacing 5 million people. Twelve years later, Haitians are still living in "tent camps" under tarps or behind pieces of carton or rusty metal with no running water, electricity, or latrines. Although these informal settlements provide temporary shelter, they are one hurricane away from being washed away.

The Framework

Located in Cap-Haitien, Haiti, this framework includes the essential infrastructure of glulam living modules, water towers, kitchens, bathrooms, and circulation. While the essential amenities are provided, the users will bring forward the infill materials according to their needs, finances, and personal tastes. By providing the essential infrastructure embedded in a solid structural foundation, these modules can enable the necessary growth and development of the community. Furthermore, the addition of communal spaces such as a market and a park on the ground floor will promote a sense of belonging and create a sense of community.

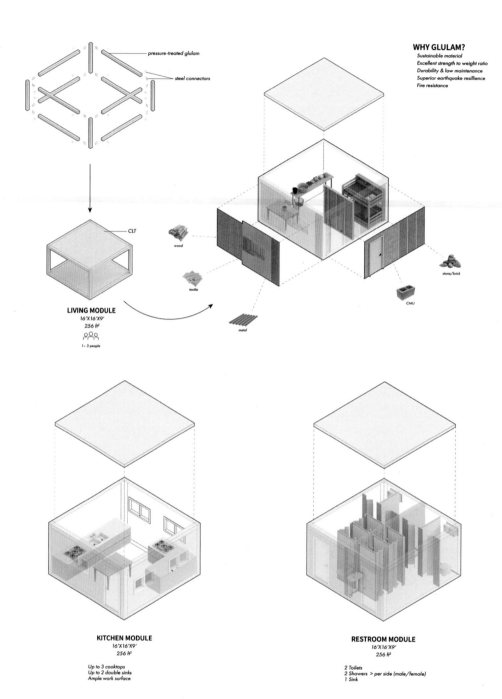

pressure-treated glulam

steel connectors

WHY GLULAM?
Sustainable material
Excellent strength to weight ratio
Durability & low maintenance
Superior earthquake resilience
Fire resistance

CLT

wood

textile

metal

stone/brick

CMU

LIVING MODULE
16'X16'X9'
256 ft²
1– 3 people

KITCHEN MODULE
16'X16'X9'
256 ft²

Up to 3 cooktops
Up to 2 double sinks
Ample work surface

RESTROOM MODULE
16'X16'X9'
256 ft²

2 Toilets
2 Showers > per side (male/female)
1 Sink

FINAL THESIS
RUNWAY REFUGE

Author: Anne Davis
Advisors: Ammar Eloueini, Cordula Roser Gray

Rural communities in the arctic region, particularly coastal villages in Alaska, are facing imminant threats such as rising sea levels and melting permafrost leading to severe erosion. These communities are currently facing the challenge of continuously fortifying their existing villages or relocating to higher ground. Although eventually unavoidable, the process of moving requires residents to break ties from the land they and their ancestors have subsisted off for centuries.

Because rural Alaskan villages do not have access to a road system, air travel serves as a lifeline to move all goods and people between villages and cities. This process is a crucial piece of rural life, as there are strong community relationships between villages; however, air travel is expensive and weather dependent. The dependence on air travel also means that importing goods and services can be very expensive, decreasing accessibility.

This thesis uses the existing infrastructure of airport landing strips as a higher ground to relocate the village of Unalakleet, Alaska, an Iñupiat community of 700 residents currently exploring relocation. In order to maintain the function of the landing strip, a new one will be lifted off of the ground with all public programs functioning underneath. The structure will house all existing public buildings as well as the addition of indoor farms to strengthen access to fresh produce.

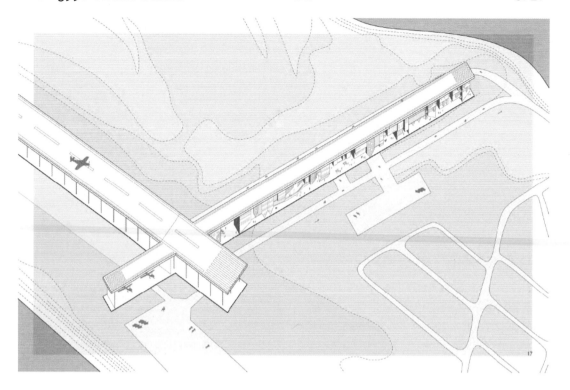

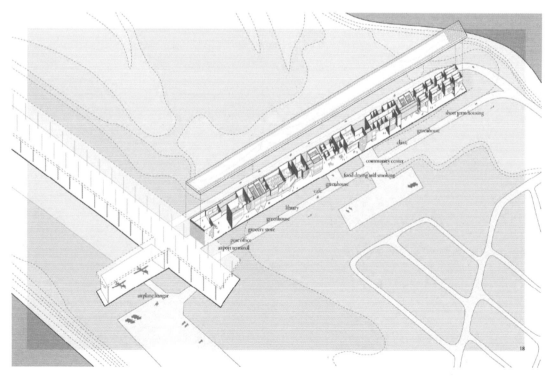

FINAL THESIS

DEGROWING LAKE CHARLES

Author: Anna Deeg
Advisors: Ammar Eloueini, Cordula Roser Gray

Degrowth Urbanism for an Ecological and Equitable Political Economy

This thesis entails both a research paper and studio design project, with the paper serving as the ideological foundation for the design project. The paper analyzes the historical and architectural implications of the capitalist-growth regime, defines and deciphers the degrowth movement through the lens of design, then culminates at the author's proposed degrowth architectural framework. The goal of the thesis is to apply the articulated architectural parameters (involving spatial strategies of sufficiency and commons with land use zoning reform) to a U.S. city. Architectural manifestos of urban utopias abound; this thesis is an attempt to bring the radical, decolonizing imaginary of degrowth from an ephemeral, elusive speculation to an attainable, abiding reality.

The Right to [Prototype] the City

Lake Charles' recent climate disasters offer a silver lining: the latent possibility to implement innovative socio-spatial practices and policies as the city rebuilds. Two blocks in downtown Lake Charles have been distinguished as a compact protoype site. Currently zoned for higher density mixed-use building types, the reality of the site is an eclectic mix of low- and high-rise buildings. The stark paucity of density and the surplus of impervious parking lots suggests a prime place for infill.

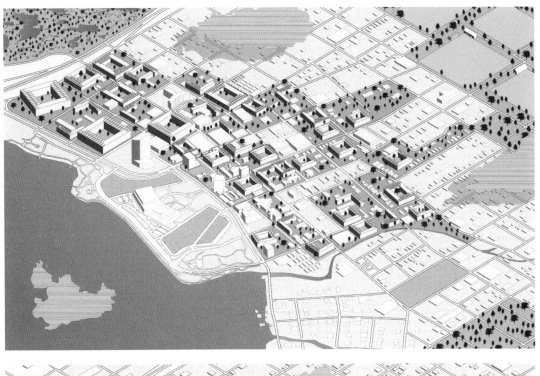

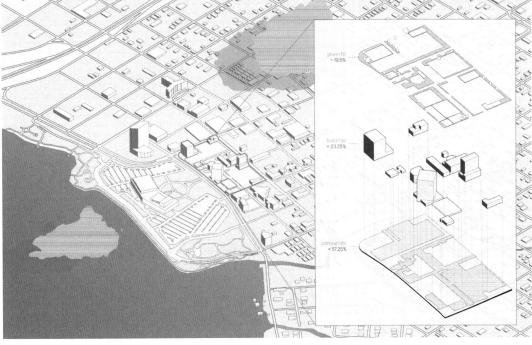

s> Anna Deeg

i> Ammar Eloueini, Cordula Roser Gray

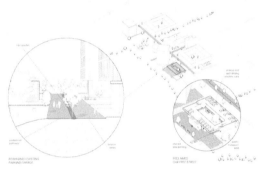

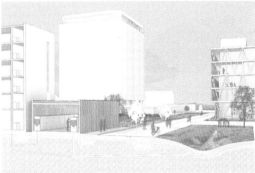

FINAL THESIS
PITI PITI

Author: Maddison Wells
Advisors: Ammar Eloueini, Cordula Roser Gray

Modularity in architecture is an attempt to increase the adaptability of the built environment by creating a structure that allows for the growth and contraction of space.

Rather than always providing a pre-assembled module, allowing the users of space to control their built environment empowers them; modular architecture has the capacity to create relatively equitable environments. The intent is to give the power of creating space back to those who have been deprived of it in the past and into the present.

The programme and site for the application of the thesis is a women and children's centre in Haiti. Instead of proposing a building, the thesis is a kit-of-parts designed and manufactured by the women of Haiti to use as they see fit.

The term Piti Piti translates to the word gradually, or little by little, in Haitian Creole. With the implementation of the Piti Piti kit-of-parts, the country of Haiti and its citizens will improve their socio-economic status over time.

The kit-of-parts is made of locally sourced, seismic-resistant materials: mycelium and bamboo. Growing and manufacturing new building materials could potentially stimulate the economy and create new sources of income, especially for women.

Rather than imposing on the existing construction techniques, the new materials are formatted as improvements to conventional building materials: CMU and rebar.

Canaan, Haiti
Lakou a (the courtyard)

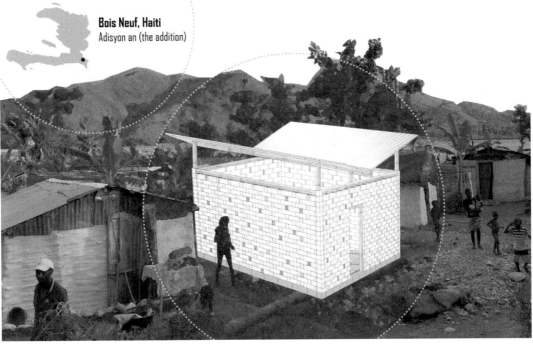

Bois Neuf, Haiti
Adisyon an (the addition)

Piti Piti : Basic Building Model
Jaden an (The Garden)

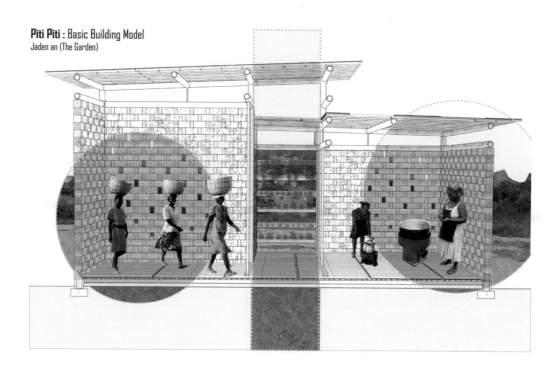

Piti Piti : Basic Building Model
Refij la (The Refuge)

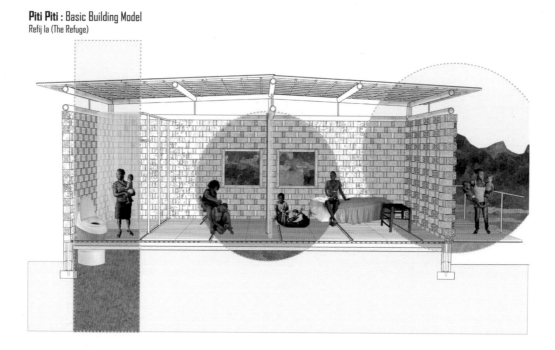

Piti Piti : Basic Building Model
Pi la (The Well)

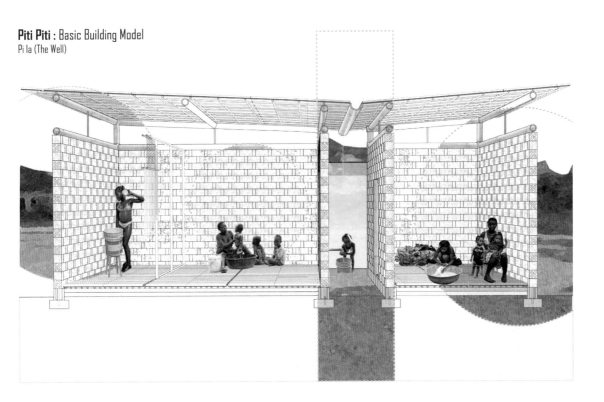

FINAL THESIS
CREATING A REGIONAL SKYSCRAPER

Author: Eitan Albukrek
Advisors: Ammar Eloueini, Cordula Roser Gray

A significant portion of modern urban development is constituted by the erection of glass and steel skyscrapers. Unlike earlier housing typologies that responded to the physical and cultural elements of their sites, these generic towers are environmentally insensitive and do not serve to capture the cultural moment of a place.

In this thesis, I aim to create a set of parameters within which contemporary skyscrapers can be designed. The parameters can be applied in any developing city but will derive unique results.

Exploring Tel Aviv, Israel, as the case study for this thesis, I set out to create a skyscraper that caters to the city's growing need for high-density residential development, while acknowledging the site's physical environment and socio-cultural context.

Built from reinforced concrete but clad in adobe sourced from the Jordan River Valley, the tower utilizes the vernacular technique of thickened walls with limited aperture area to achieve cool, low-impact interiors.

Connected by a secondary circulation path, a series of shared amenity spaces are articulated on the tower's facade as vaulted openings. In combination with a public, vaulted ground floor area, these semi-public spaces reference historical neighbourhood courtyards, emulating the organization and built culture of historical Middle Eastern villages.

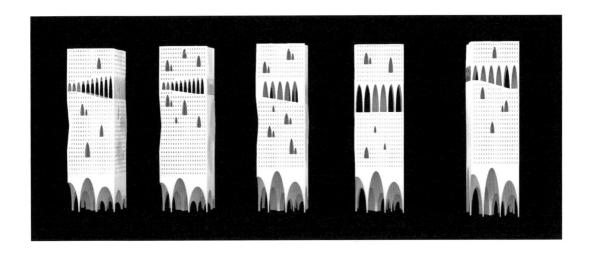

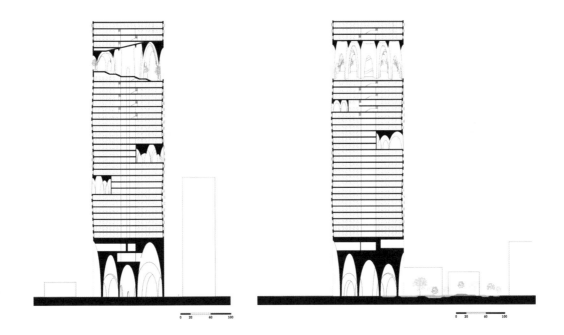

FINAL THESIS
POST-INDUSTRIAL CHICAGO RIVER

Author: Evan Warder
Advisor: Iñaki Alday

Urban centers around the world have witnessed the disappearance of the industry that once defined their livelihood. Rivers were often the structural elements that allowed prosperity for industrial cities, but as the industry depleted, the core values of the rivers were lost. Chicago, a city founded on the notion of industrial capabilities and its placement along a river, struggles with this identity crisis. Like many cities, Chicago has changed its attitude toward the river from a shipping asset and sewer, to a space for experiencing nature and leisure in a dense urban environment.

The Pilsen Industrial Corridor is still clearly defined by an industrial framework. The Fisk Generating Plant is a lasting scar of the former industry, a major coal power plant that was closed in response to its polluting nature. The redevelopment of this site will have a significant impact socially and politically, giving it an opportunity to anchor the positive future of the industrial corridor. As the citizens fight against gentrification today, the need for new jobs is exacerbated by growing populations and declining productivity. As the city continues to grow,

access to reliable food systems has become a luxury more than an expectation. The destruction of the fishing industry and the expense of importing all produce has removed the ability for many residents to buy and eat fresh food.

The varying approaches to post-industrial development in the last three decades have been one dimensional. Cities that have attempted comprehensive plans for these sites have focused on commercial development, parks, cultural centers, technology districts, or continuing productivity, but these rarely overlap.

Chicago presents the opportunity to combine several of these approaches through reinvestment in productivity, providing jobs and needed food through high-density vertical farming and aquaculture. Productive space combined with a school, market, café, shared kitchen, and restaurant provide extensive value to the communities without risking their ability to continue to inhabit their neighborhood.

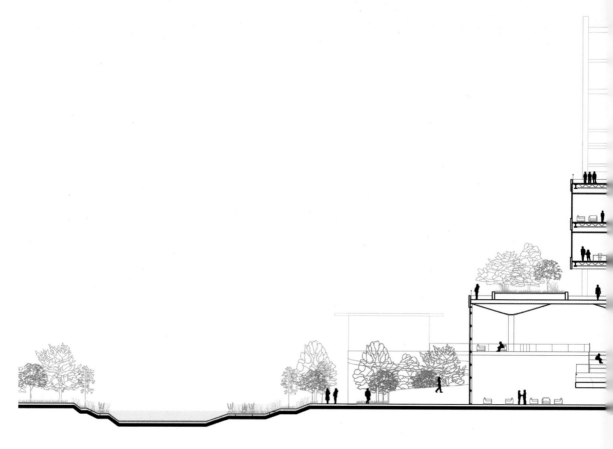

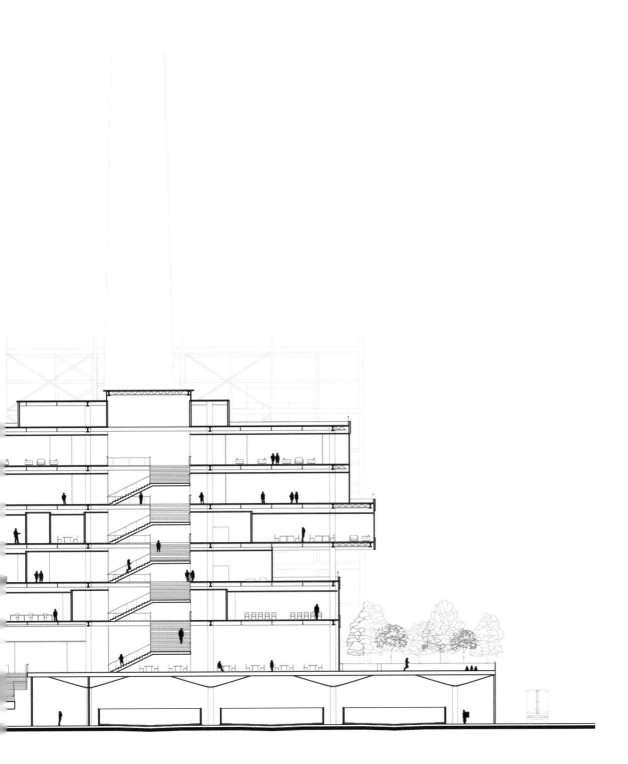

FINAL THESIS
NO ROYAL ROADS

Author: Charles Jones
Advisor: Kentaro Tsubaki

Smoothness is a technical overcorrection in designing and constructing various urban street typologies. The singular pursuit of achieving smoothness in urban street surfaces, in the past and present, has inhibited the development of more resilient and ecologically adaptive solutions. These possible solutions are now fundamental to the long-term sustainability of low-lying, coastal urban centers with greater exposure risk to aging subsurface infrastructure, subsidence, and episodic flooding.

Most paving standards and specifications for city streets trickle down from federal highway paving standards which rightfully privilege efficient vehicular travel. However, city streets do not support the same vehicular traffic demand. In fact, they have supported a slower-paced space for pedestrians to be in, rather than move through, for centuries.

The sectional profile of the crown finds its origins in paved roads dating back to the Roman empire, when the sole purpose was to shed water efficiently. This characteristic is more flexible thanks to the aid of subsurface drainage networks. The rapid discharge of water, another heroic modern feat, is now seen as a detriment in cities like New Orleans, where paving systems rupture due to unbalanced groundwater conditions and soil heaving. Lastly, hydrophobic material properties are more favorable to asphalt, a bituminous descendant known for its ability to waterproof vessels, which is preferred for its ability to reduce moisture absorption.

This focus is maladaptive in addressing the rising social and ecological pressures streets face in coastal cities like New Orleans. Local streets make up 69% of all city-owned streets in New Orleans and are the focus of intervention within the scope framework of the current $2.3 billion road reconstruction project. This means that about 30% of the entire city streetscape is being reconstructed with the same century-old, impermeable technology. This thesis proposes more adaptive considerations, that focus less on smoothness, should be incorporated into the process of redesigning street paving systems and their spatial configuration.

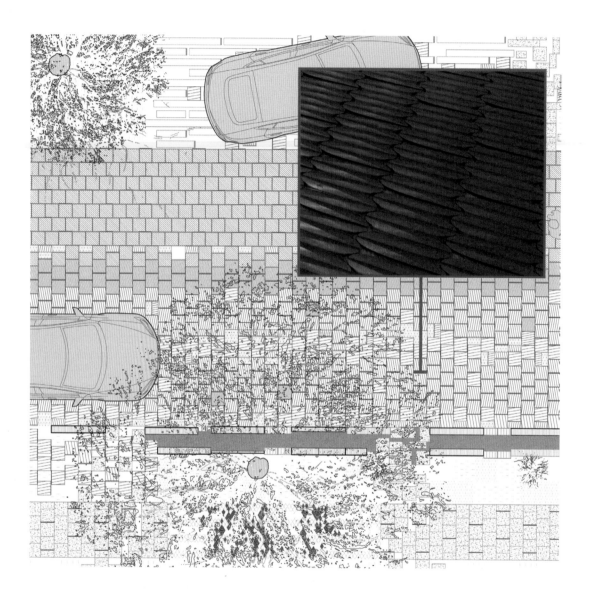

FINAL THESIS
REGENERATIVE HABITAT

Author: Gabrielle Rashleigh
Advisor: Margarita Jover

"Regenerative Habitat" offers a spatial test for a climate-adaptive urban model in the face of rising seas, coastal land loss, and increased storm frequency along the Gulf Coast. The project centers on the Bayou Bienvenue Central Wetland Unit, located between Orleans and St. Bernard Parish in Louisiana. Over the course of the past century, this heavily engineered site has converted from a freshwater baldcypress and water tupelo swamp to open water, leaving the adjacent neighborhoods vulnerable to storm surges.

Bayou Bienvenue Central Wetland Unit occupies a coveted space within the Hurricane and Storm Damage Risk Reduction system. As climate change pressures coastal populations to relocate to protected higher grounds, the site, today an urban backyard, offers a location to temporarily absorb climate change refugees — inside of the levee walls and outside of the subsiding low grounds of New Orleans. Additionally, the site puts forth a model for inhabiting a floodable landscape without relying on the pump system that has exacerbated subsidence in New Orleans.

This thesis proposes three strategies for amplifying the ecological and social wealth of the Central Wetland Unit and surrounding neighborhood through marsh terracing, elevated urbanism, and regenerative practices and infrastructures.

Marsh terracing, currently utilized in Louisiana to stabilize coastal land loss, employs a simple cut and fill operation to build up land for marshes. Elevated urbanism proposes a method for inhabiting wetlands without draining the vital groundwater by lifting both utilities and buildings onto piers, forming an interconnected 'mat-building'. Lastly, regenerative practices and infrastructures put forth a form of inhabitation that links urban and ecological metabolisms into a mutualistic and symbiotic relationship. These practices include: an extensive rainwater collection system for irrigating select marsh terraces with fresh water to foster biodiversity, a harvesting system for organic waste processed for biogas and compost, a network of microgrids for solar energy production, fields for orchards, and aquaculture with oysters and tilapia.

FINAL THESIS
PRODUCTIVE MATRIX

Author: Théa Spring
Advisor: Iñaki Alday

On the eastern edge of Paris, in the commune of Montreuil, there sits a landscape called the *Murs à Pêches*. The 10-foot walls striating its soil have existed since the mid-17th century. Built and maintained as an agricultural tool, they shielded winds and stocked heat to provide the plots with a microclimate 45 to 50 degrees warmer than the surrounding area. As Parisian demand for fruits and vegetables grew through the 18th and 19th centuries, a complex and experimental system was developed by the Montreuillois combining horticulture, viticulture, and arboriculture. By the end of the 18th century, the area of the *Murs à Pêches* reached its apogee with over 300 hectares of walled lots — one-third of Montreuil.

Today, the remaining 30 hectares survive as an enclave between programmatically specialized zones of the Paris *banlieue*. For unfamiliar Parisians, the half-ruined walls look like imminent victims to residential development. For others, the *Murs à Pêches*'s preservation is imagined as a kind of soft horticultural museumification. Yet, in the last few decades, the ambiguous identity of this half-forgotten territory has proven to be very generative for a diverse range of cultural, educational, social, and economic activities.

This thesis proposes a further evolution of the *Murs à Pêches* into a dense metabolic and agricultural urbanity. Informed by the land's historic logics of production, cultural history, and contemporary urban needs of surrounding *banlieues*, strategic public space interventions and metabolic elements are designed to structure and power a new kind of productive landscape. Though the *Murs à Pêches* is rich in singularities, many of its social, economic, and environmental issues are widely common in other parts of Grand Paris and other extended metropolises. This thesis is driven by a desire to explore the constructive tensions between site specificity and broader social and environmental urgencies, as they will be arguably central to architecture for the years to come.

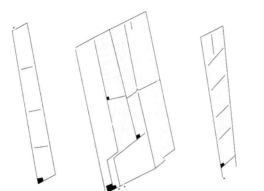

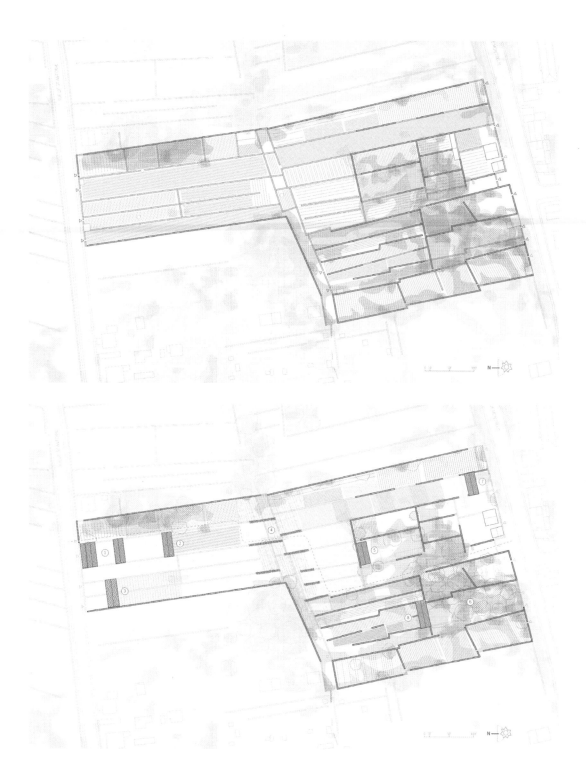

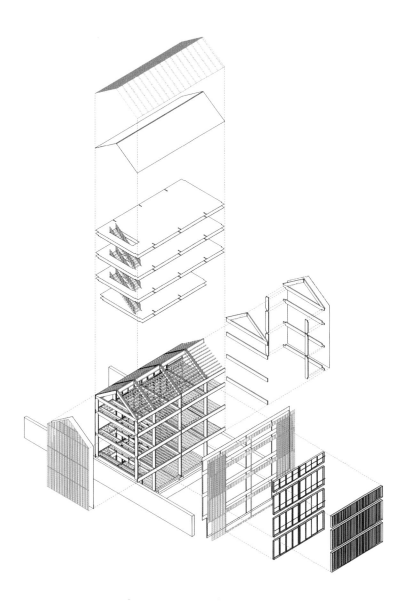

what for

faculty work

Rubén García Rubio & Sonsoles Vela

Day Care Center for People with Alzheimer's Disease

CIVIC BUILDING
Zamora, Spain; 2008-2020

The new Day Care Center for People with Alzheimer's Disease in Benavente (Zamora, Spain) arises from the aging of the region's population. When designed, there was no proven scheme for this typology, despite the growth of the disease in recent years in some regions of the country. Hence, the initial program only specified the inclusion of spaces for cognitive and physical stimulation activities, with a dining and rest area for 50 users. Therefore, the first task was to understand the logic of this typology and crystallize it into an architectural scheme.

Another important starting point was the location of the center within a double-boundary situation (territorial and urban). On the one hand, the town is located on the periphery of the great Castilian plateau, so it is endowed with a particular topography: between hills, valleys, and plains, with a historical condition of crossing roads, and some of the main arterial roads of the country. On the other hand, the plot is also located within a municipal boundary area, on a hill with a steep slope between an expansion area and farmland. This situation emphasizes the conjunction of landscapes in the building again.

These ideas motivated the positioning of the building in the upper part of the plot to facilitate a stratum of it to rotate and tear the slope to create a new plain area. Then, in a second movement, part of that stratum rises another level vertically to protect the building on its urban front. Thus, a new line of the horizon is created, the main subject of the building, which not only symbolizes the synergy of the community in the face of this disease but also dialogues with the landscape.

Once on the surface, the emerging stratum is excavated to house the different spaces. These are divided into four zones according to their degrees of privacy and use. Primarily,, two large retaining walls extend outwards to mark the entrance and separate the public spaces (differentiated as administrative and multipurpose areas) from the

CREDITS

Architects
Rubén García Rubio
Sonsoles Vela Navarro
studioVRA

Photography
Javier Bravo Fotografía
Rubén García Rubio

private ones. Simultaneously,, the latter spaces are articulated around two corridors of generous width, which
diversity assists in spatially orienting visitors. These spaces
are conceived as the most important "rooms" with the-
rapeutic functioning in the center. The rest of the private
spaces can be accessed from each of them. One provides
access to the most frequently used rooms (classrooms,
geriatric bathrooms, courtyards), and the other to the
lesser-used spaces (dining area, rest area). All of them are
designed according to the specific needs of people with
Alzheimer's disease. Thus, it is designed with a clear and
forceful scheme that optimizes the operation of the building, allowing for simple, simultaneous, and independent
use of the different areas and a maximized use of its energy resources.

A great significance is given to the design elements inside
the building. These details help qualify the space and make
it more recognizable and comfortable for the user. For
example, the continuity of the railings in the corridors, the
courtyards (classrooms) that allow inhabitants to engage
in activities while in clean air and natural lighting, or the
use of materials that improve the comfort of the user and
the use of the center. In this sense, the classrooms gain
importance for their position and the use of the large windows that connect the excavated space to the landscape.

The rest of the plot – developing in a second phase – is
a large two-level garden. However, both levels are conceived together due to their common conceptual origin,
and the upper garden extends itself over the green roof
and water storage. Hence, the building is related to the
landscape, both formally and materially. This area is conceived as the largest room in the center, as it encourages
outdoor activities and assures users direct contact with
the outside and the landscape of their memory.

Fig. 1 (Above)
Second floor plan.

Fig. 2 (Below)
Section view.

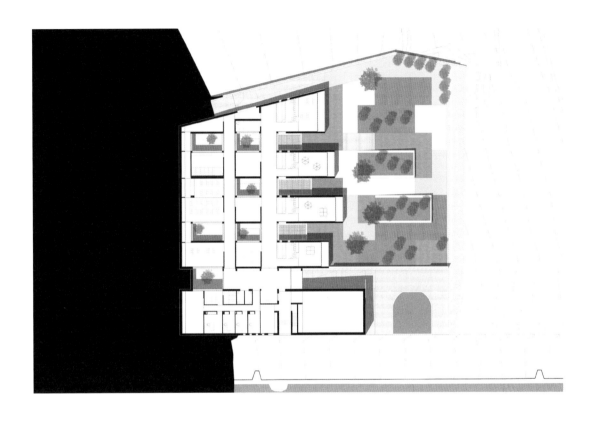

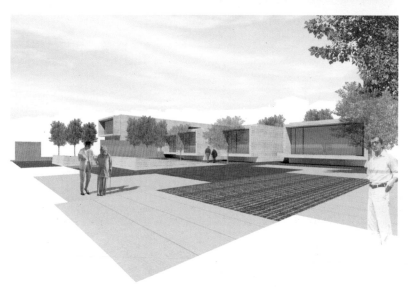

Fig. 3, 4, 5 (Left)
Collages:
Interior Corridor
Interior Courtyard
Exterior Yard

Fig. 6, 7 (Right)
Final photos.

Irene Keil & David Gregor

The Tulane Bead Tree

INSTALLATION
New Orleans, Louisiana, 2020-2022

As a temporary replacement for the original Nuttall Oak bead tree on the Tulane campus, three tree-like structures are placed in an area close to the original. They are fabricated from a 6-inch diameter weathered black iron pipe, each reaching a height of 21 feet. A forest of steel branches and twigs has been drilled into these trunks, allowing for the catching of beads. In addition, a series of clear plexiglass rods penetrate the pipe, from which light emanates during evening hours. Finally, the three elements sit within a shape, emulating the outline of the former canopy. This shape is edged in steel, filled with a thin layer of fine red gravel.

CREDITS

Design & Fabrication
David Gregor
Irene Keil

Installation
Demian Weidenhaft
Robert Pourciau
Tulane Facilities

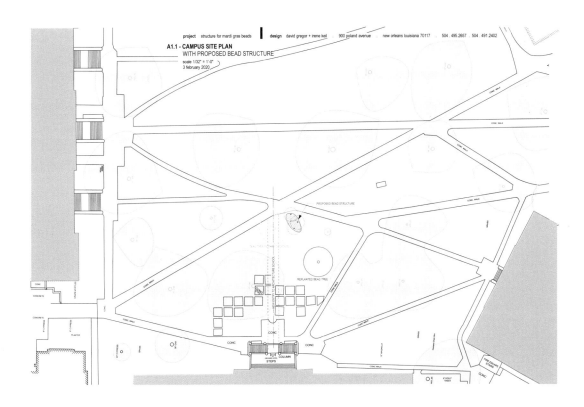

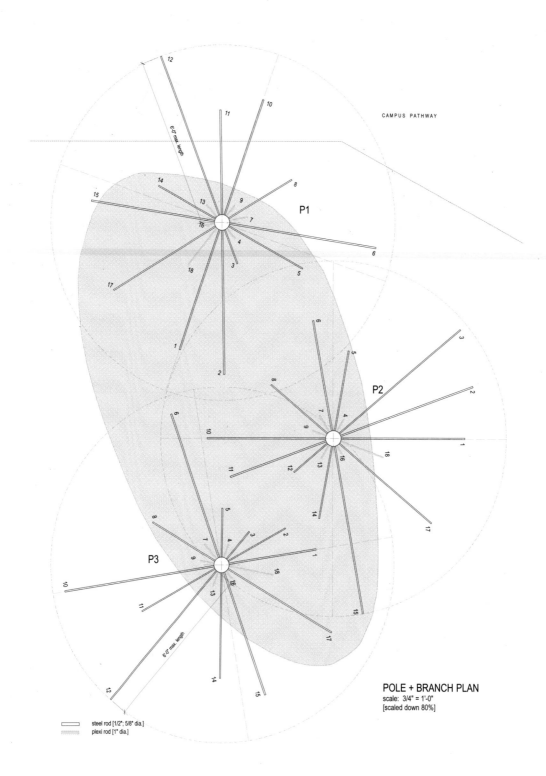

CAMPUS PATHWAY

P1

P2

P3

6'-0" max length

6'-0" max length

POLE + BRANCH PLAN
scale: 3/4" = 1'-0"
[scaled down 80%]

steel rod [1/2"; 5/8" dia.]
plexi rod [1" dia.]

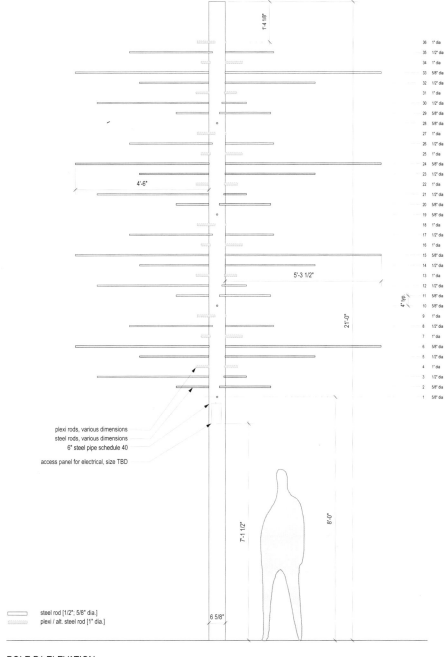

36	1" dia
35	1/2" dia
34	1" dia
33	5/8" dia
32	1/2" dia
31	1" dia
30	1/2" dia
29	5/8" dia
28	5/8" dia
27	1" dia
26	1/2" dia
25	1" dia
24	5/8" dia
23	1/2" dia
22	1" dia
21	1/2" dia
20	5/8" dia
19	5/8" dia
18	1" dia
17	1/2" dia
16	1" dia
15	5/8" dia
14	1/2" dia
13	1" dia
12	1/2" dia
11	5/8" dia
10	5/8" dia
9	1" dia
8	1/2" dia
7	1" dia
6	5/8" dia
5	1/2" dia
4	1" dia
3	1/2" dia
2	5/8" dia
1	5/8" dia

1'-4 1/8"

4'-6"

5'-3 1/2"

4" typ.

21'-0"

plexi rods, various dimensions
steel rods, various dimensions
6" steel pipe schedule 40

access panel for electrical, size TBD

7'-1 1/2"

8'-0"

6 5/8"

steel rod [1/2"; 5/8" dia.]
plexi / alt. steel rod [1" dia.]

POLE P1 ELEVATION
scale: 3/4" = 1'-0"
[scaled by 80%]

356

Fig. 1 (Previous Page)
Plan, elevation.

Fig. 2, 3, 4 (First Column)
Fabrication

Fig. 5, 6, 7 (Second Column)
Installation

Fig. 4 (Above)
Finished Installation

what for   Faculty Work   357

Carrie Norman

NOTRE

COMMERCIAL BUILDING
Chicago, IL; 2018-2019

The renovation of Notre's storefront in Chicago's Fulton-Randolph Market draws its inspiration, and challenges, from two histories: one distant, one immediate. The space is located on the first floor of the 1906 Edward Katzinger & Company Building, once a manufacturer of tin pans for commercial bakeries. Two giant street-facing entryways and a three-foot grade change indicate the space once served as a loading dock. More recently, the space was home to Rhona Hoffman, a prominent commercial art gallery known for representing critical artists like Michael Rakowitz, Torkwase Dyson, and Jenny Holzer. The existing conditions conveyed a high contrast between a white wall gallery and a massive heavy timber structure with exposed mechanical and fire safety systems. Notre aims to replace its warehouse-gallery origins with a domestic enfilade, or series of intimately interconnected low-ceiling rooms that accommodate varied products — clothing, footwear, publications, apothecary — and varied events — reading, lecture, and transaction.

Upon entering through Notre's 13-feet tall door, you are tasked with entering the store a second time: although inside, you are still outside. Four gentle slopes mediated by low-rise steps are clad by 4,645 Chicago common brick pavers, sourced from a local brickyard. The multi-purpose stair-ramp (or "stramp") provides an accessible entry to a previously inaccessible space, as well as integrates custom furniture to transform it from circulation into a theater of 80 seats. The store proper is pushed inside and away from the street, where a two-feet systems. Here, one-foot timber columns are sandwiched between thickened walls and open-door jambs. The resultant rooms are connected only through passing views. A new sense of retail intimacy is drawn. Notre's renovation revels in its ability to combine social pragmatism with aesthetic appeal. Like the inclusive culture it supports, Notre does not believe the two are mutually exclusive.

CREDITS

Architects
Norman Kelley

Design Team
Isabelle Reford
Abigail Chang
Benjamin Gott

Photography
Chris Leh

Renovation Plan (+4'-0")

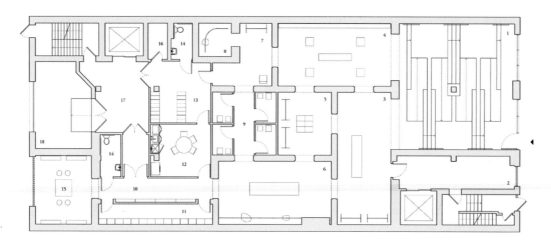

1. Vestibule (Stair-Ramp)	6. High-Fashion	11. Storage	16. Storage
2. Elevator Lobby	7. Streetwear	12. Break Room	17. Receiving Room
3. Point of Sale	8. Streetwear Vault	13. Storage	18. Loading Dock
4. Footwear	9. Fitting Rooms	14. Restroom	
5. Build-Out	10. Apothecary	15. Publications	

Finish Plan (+4'-0")

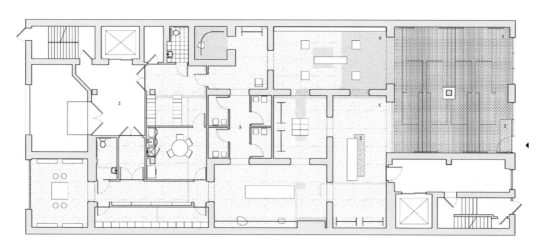

1. Brick
2. Cocomat
3. Carpet
4. New Concrete
5. Existing Concrete

Fig. 1 (Left, Above)
Renovation plan.

Fig. 2 (Left, Below)
Finish plan.

Fig. 3 (Below)
Storefront axonometric.

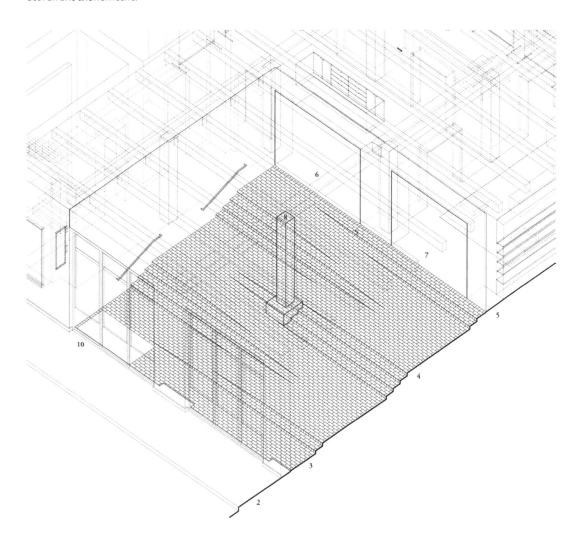

Following pages:
Fig. 4 (Left)
Interior views.

Fig. 5 (Right)
Interior entry, various lighting conditions.

The ReView

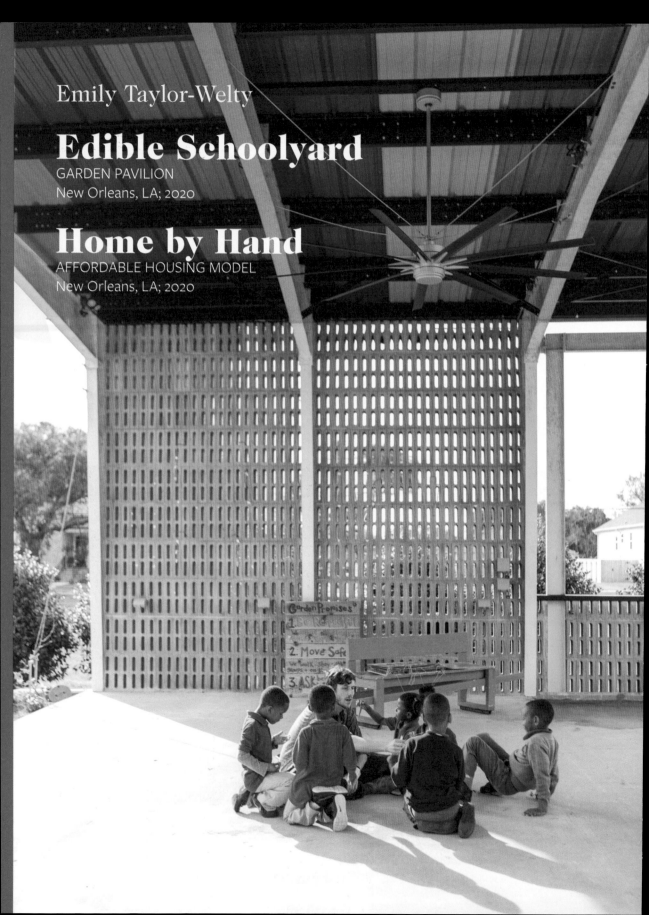

Emily Taylor-Welty

Edible Schoolyard
GARDEN PAVILION
New Orleans, LA; 2020

Home by Hand
AFFORDABLE HOUSING MODEL
New Orleans, LA; 2020

Emilie Taylor Welty, a professor of practice at Tulane's School of Architecture has a New Orleans-based firm called Colectivo. The firm has designed numerous award-winning projects across the South and their typical work is in residential and small-scale commercial projects. The firm's research and design is grounded in making — which can be seen in high-end project details. It also comes to bear when collaborating with builders to devise replicable energy-efficient housing to address the affordable housing crisis in the city.

CREDITS

Architects
Colectivo

Photography
Michael Wong

Fig. 1 (Left)
Edible Schoolyard pavilion.

Fig. 2 (Above)
Pavilion render.

THE EDIBLE SCHOOLYARD

Colectivo designed the Oak Park Garden Pavilion and Accessory Landscape Structures for Arthur Ashe Charter School in New Orleans. The goal was to create an outdoor classroom pavilion and supporting garden spaces for teachers, students, and the surrounding neighborhood.

The Edible Schoolyard Garden Pavilion and Greenhouse is located on a linear site between Arthur Ashe Charter School and Oak Park. The site is bracketed by two major program components, the greenhouse and the pavilion, which are linked with a central circulation spine. The central walkway is populated with multiple louvered trellis structures that serve as teaching "nodes." These help activate the walkway and divide the site into different planting zones. Each trellis structure is designed to be planted out with climbing vines. The walkway culminates at the pavilion, which is raised about three feet, introducing grade changes that encourage different types of site hydrology. The pavilion is surrounded by a series of terraced planter beds where students get hands-on access to the herbs and fruit trees, and are encouraged to climb through the beds as they learn about the plants.

While the garden structure primarily serves classes of students during the day, it is also meant to be open to the community and encourage neighbors to use the garden and pavilion for parties and social gatherings. The pavilion utilizes a prefabricated structure as a nod to vernacular urban park structures, and as a way to explore new articulations of industrial building types. The project was designed and built as a joint venture between Colectivo and Appropriate Technologies.

Fig. 3 (Above)
Zoning diagram for non-structural components.

Fig. 4 (Below)
Pavilion entrance.

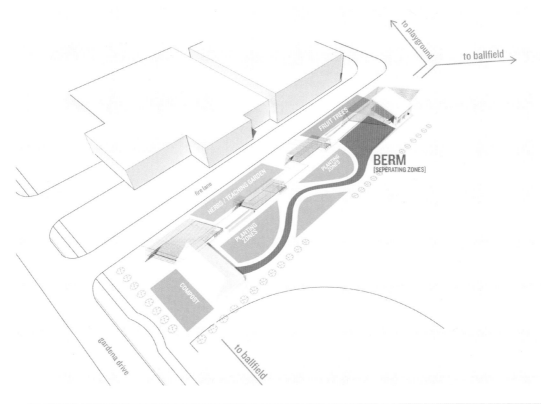

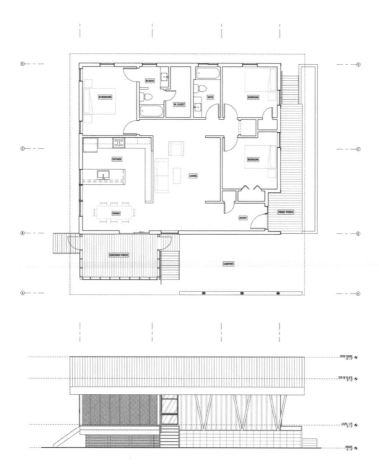

HOME BY HAND

Home ownership in the U.S. is a way to build generational wealth, to root families in a place, and to stabilize their housing costs in a way that improves the quality of life. Yet, in cities, the price of housing is increasingly at odds with average median incomes, pushing working-class families further away from job centers and exacerbating income inequality. In an effort to combat these forces and create scores of affordable homes in New Orleans neighborhoods, a developer (Home by Hand) teamed up with a design firm (Colectivo) and contractor (TKTMJ) to rethink the housing delivery model to ensure that families have access to well-designed, energy-efficient affordable housing. The project, Home by Hand, borrows from the self-help housing model that grew out of 1960's New York. Home by Hand combines that with early stage cooperation between builders and architects to design for climate, market, and neighborhood nuances of New Orleans, to produce affordable and high quality homes.

With each housing model prototype and subsequent iteration, the design team and contractor work alongside each other to identify opportunities to streamline the material and detailing efficiencies. They also work with past home owners to identify spatial and material opportunities to improve the quality of the designs. What has developed out of this body of research and collaboration is a design strategy which blends the local porch culture and contextual design with pragmatism in layout and detailing.

Fig. 5 (Above, Left)
Plan, elevation. 1 of 5 unique models.

Fig. 6 (Below, Left)
6 of 25 built homes.

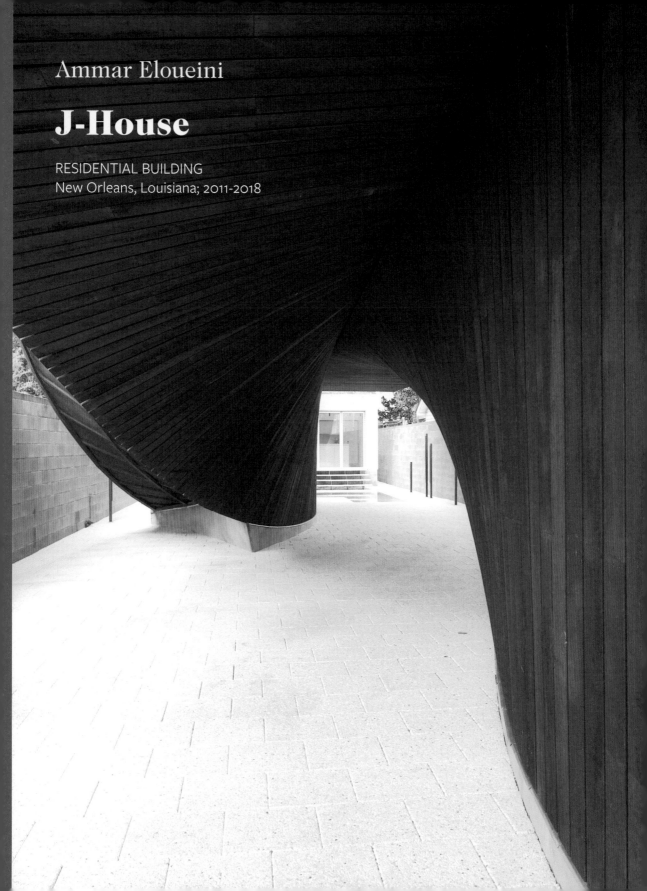

Ammar Eloueini

J-House

RESIDENTIAL BUILDING
New Orleans, Louisiana; 2011-2018

After four years in design, three different locations, two permits, and a zoning variance from the city of New Orleans, the construction on the J-House started on January 24, 2011 and was completed in 2018.

The J-House is a speculative residence in the heart of historic New Orleans. It uses a historically standard New Orleans housing lot (30x150 feet). The design responds to the context by elevating the main living area ten feet above ground. Most of New Orleans is several feet below sea level and prone to frequent flooding.

The design uses a steel structure to create a bridge-like structure that allows a minimal footprint and can resist 180 mph hurricane winds. The outside is clad with rain-in-screen charred cedar planks that help prevent heat transmission during summer heat waves and offer resilience to notorious termite damage in the region.

While unusually formal in comparison to its surroundings, the J-House outside wood cladding tends to bring the project back to the domestic realm.

The J-House responds to local climate conditions in how it is situated and by the materials used for its construction. It is also a study of place, constraints, and possibilities. The J-House was inspired by the shotgun house typology; a housing stock that typifies New Orleans. It is also part of a lineage of speculative houses designed since the early 20th century to redefine preconceived notions and ideas of domesticity.

CREDITS

Architects
Ammar Eloueini Digit-all Studio

Photographs
Richard Schulman
Ammar Eloueini
Nick LiCausi

Fig. 2 (Left, Above)
Skylight, main stairs.

Fig. 3 (Left, Below)
Living space and kitchen.

Fig. 4 (Right, Above)
2nd, 1st Floor plans.

Fig. 5 (Right, Below)
Longitudinal sections.

The ReView

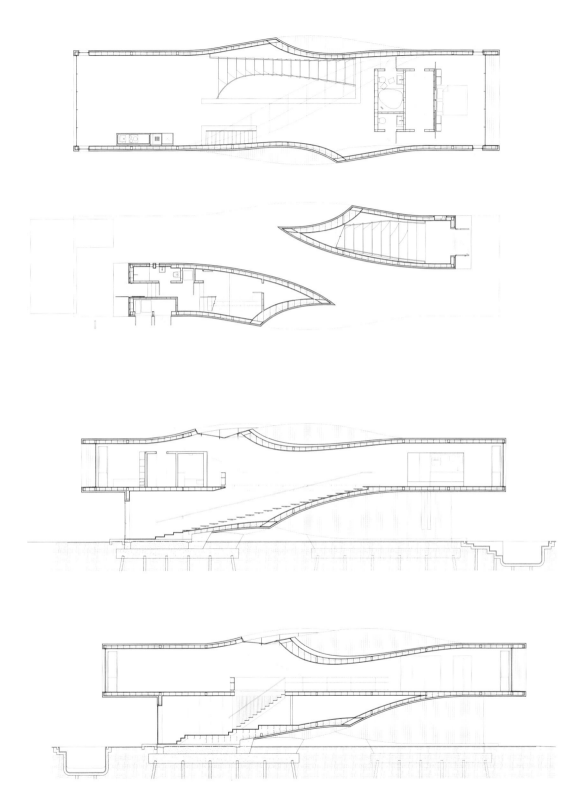

374

Fig. 4 (Above)
Drone views in context.

Fig. 5 (Left)
Living space, overlooking
guest house.

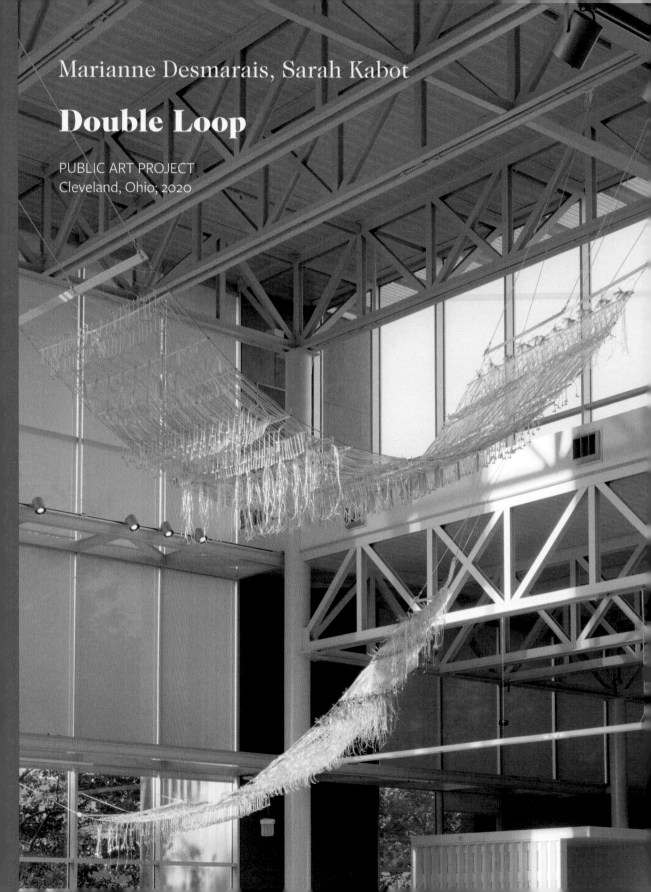

Marianne Desmarais, Sarah Kabot

Double Loop

PUBLIC ART PROJECT
Cleveland, Ohio; 2020

In 2020, Sarah Kabot and Marianne Desmarais were commissioned to create a piece of public artwork from the medical waste stream at the Cleveland Clinic. The work, titled Double Loop, responded to a joint initiative directed by the Clinic's Arts and Medicine Institute and the Office for a Healthy Environment to collaborate in revisioning a future that centers well-being. These efforts strive to create operational practices that stop waste and reduce chemical use to improve the stewardship of built and natural environments.

The commissioned artwork emerges from plastic offcasts at the clinic both physically and conceptually. Unused, but expired, medical supplies such as tubing from infusion kits and pipet trays form the textural components of the work. Beyond intended use, these items exist outside typical pathways for reclamation and cannot be used by other clinics or hospitals where supplies are desperately needed. Double Loop redefines these plastic objects by amplifying their material characteristics to surprise and delight. The project reconceptualized waste streams of material culture by taking the position that to alter wasteful processes, observation of the qualities and characteristics of all residuals is necessary.

Inherent qualities of strength and flexibility allowed many textile production techniques to be utilized to construct the two tensile arcs that comprise Double Loop. Over 200 pounds of plastic are affixed to architectural, stainless-steel cable-mesh that hangs from custom hardware in the structural undercroft of the roof. Attachment methods vary from direct connections to gathered units of extended fringe and draped loops on steel tube stretchers.

Detangling memories from the visual presence of these single-use objects required defamiliarizing the familiar to provoke new relationships and alter perception around the sensorial experience of bodies in health care. Exposing the fiber optic qualities of tubing, each composite textile

CREDITS

Design, Installation
Sarah Kabot
Marianne Desmarais

Photographs
Joseph Minek

transposes light across a diaphanous surface. Color shifts combined with the viewer's movement around the work yield fluid experiences with multiple vantage points. Repositioning the physical properties of plastic medical materials connects directly with the dislocating experience of illness and care in pieces that float in public space.

Working with the Office for a Healthy Environment to repurpose these discards is conceptually and ecologically engaging. Designed to be in suspension, Double Loop hangs from the building structure to float in the visual field of Healthspace forty feet above the floor. The environment of the Cleveland Clinic embodies the principles of care and innovation. Double Loop echoes this spirit of the site, inspired by the meeting of human culture, the biological environment, and the materiality of scientific work.

Fig. 1 (Right)
Detail view of textile.

Following pages:
Fig. 2 (Left)
Detail view of textile.

Fig. 3 (Above)
Textile installation at the
Zeliony Institute.

The ReView

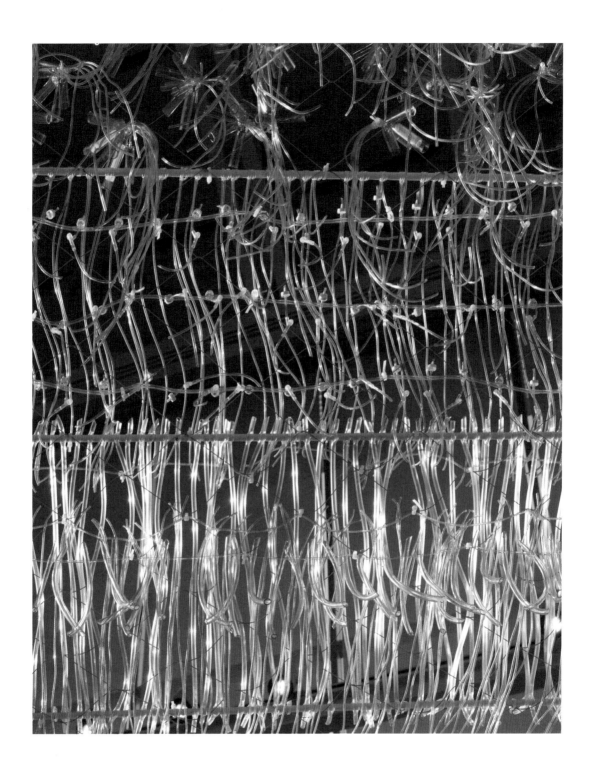

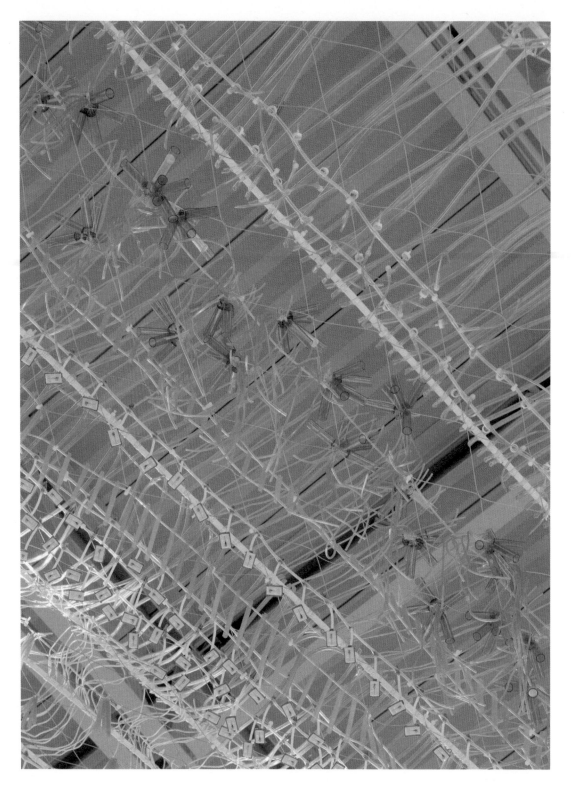

The ReView

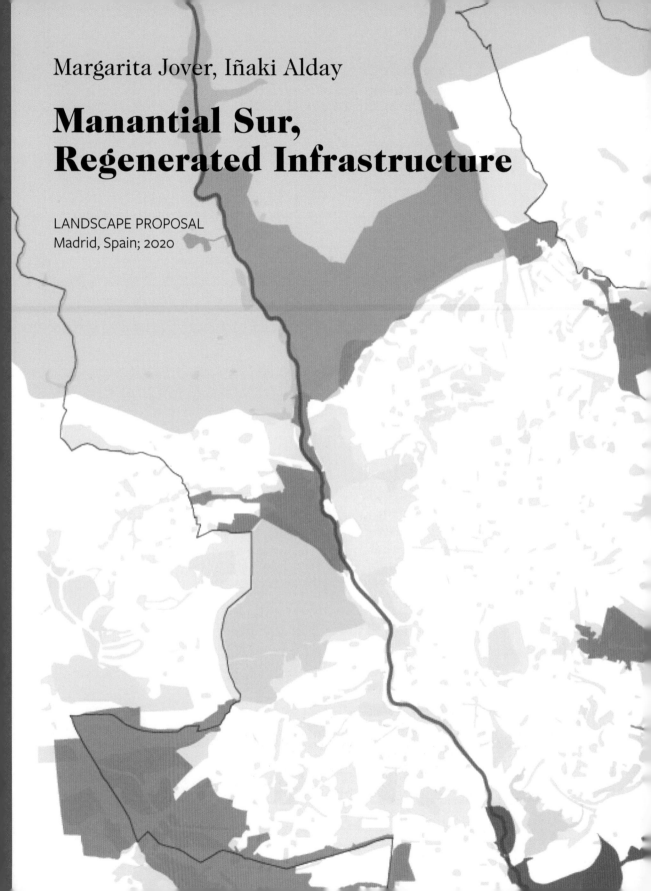

Margarita Jover, Iñaki Alday

Manantial Sur, Regenerated Infrastructure

LANDSCAPE PROPOSAL
Madrid, Spain; 2020

aldayjover architecture and landscape's proposal has been chosen as the winner of the Madrid Metropolitan Forest International Contest, Lot 4 "The Southern River Parks". A jury made up of 24 experts selected Manantial Sur, Re-generated Infrastructure for being a "complete project in all its components that has generated debate around the role of water, forestry and agriculture."

The southern area of Madrid, along the Manzanares Ri-ver, is a place of infrastructures that have divided the te-rritory; but it is also a space of opportunities and full of latent resources: hydrological, historical, agricultural, hor-ticultural, archaeological, and social to be enhanced and to re-sprout.

aldayjover changed the discourse in the relationship be-tween rivers and cities by designing the first floodable pu-blic spaces, conceived as hybrid hydraulic infrastructures, at the end of the 1990s. In the Manantial Sur of the Me-tropolitan Forest, aldayjover reconceptualizes the artificial hydrology of the region, complementing the sources of fresh water from the Sierra de Madrid with the new water springs – the wastewater treatment plants. This concept, initially developed for Delhi (Yamuna River Project, with Pankaj Vir Gupta), will generate a new landscape that ma-nages water and nature, creates microclimates, promotes healthy habits, and is the backbone of a more equitable and democratic society based on the right to quality pu-blic space.

Manantial Sur is a proposal for social and ecological grow-th. The social resprout recovers pedestrian connectivity and creates civic centralities. The ecological resprout pro-motes the emergence of biodiversity and a large monu-mental forest based on better use and management of water resources. The resprout of mobility infrastructures comes from understanding them as broad ecological co-rridors that include slow mobility and creates an agrofo-restry and social mosaic.

CREDITS

Architects
Iñaki Alday
Margarita Jover
Jesús Arcos
Francisco Mesonero

Developed from a transdisciplinary perspective, aldayjover in collaboration with ABM Consulting, IRBIS ecological consulting, Paisaje Transversal, Benedicto Gestión de Proyectos, BIS structures, and fdTOP has led this proposal in Madrid's green belt, which will become the first major metropolitan intervention to mitigate the effects of climate change in the capital of Spain. A forest that was born attentive to the increasingly pressing social and ecological challenges, using water as a driving force for planning and design.

Fig. 1 (Right)
Landscape interventions, perspective views.

Fig. 2 (Below)
Principal habitats.

Fig. 3 (Following pages)
Vista view in entirety.

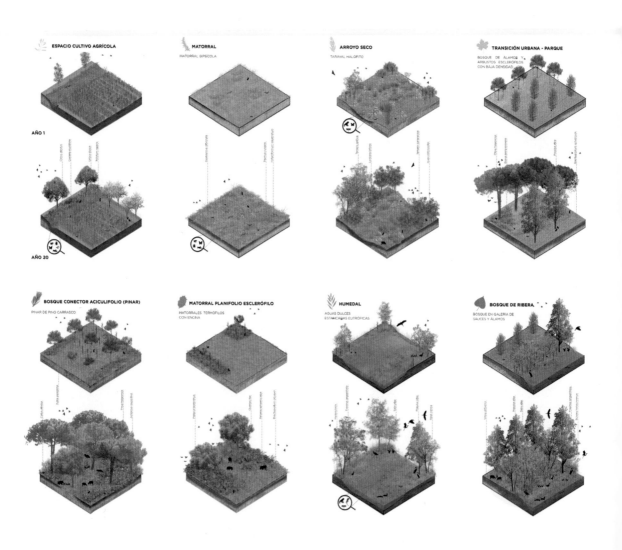

The ReView

The ReView

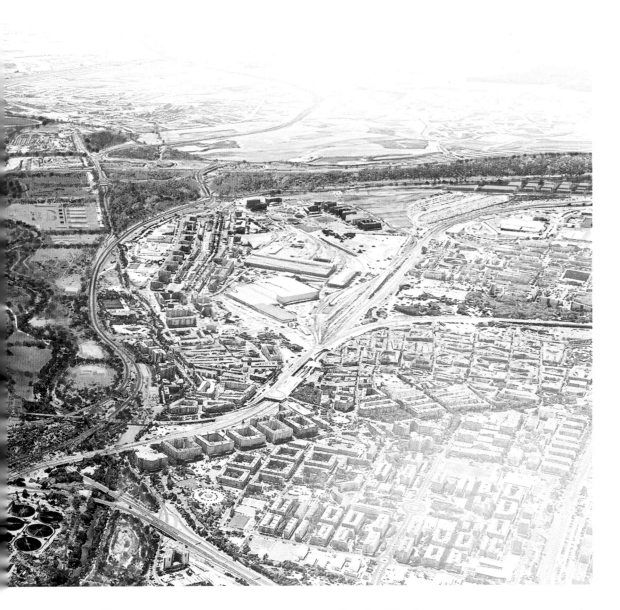

LECTURES
& EVENTS

STUDENT EXHIBITS

New Visual Identity
Pentagram Design [September 2020]

Sukkah 12
Seth Laskin, undergraduate student
(coordinator) and Sukkah 2020 team
[October 2020]

Freehand Drawing and Observations
Andrew Liles, Adjunct Assistant Lecturer
[October 2020]

URBANBuild
Byron Mouton, Senior Professor
of Practice [November 2020]

Building Preservation Studio Tomb
Ellen Feringa, graduate student
[January 2021]

Small Center Design/Build Fall 2020
[Feburary 2021]

Undergraduate Design Symposium
[March 2021]

Choose Wisely
Jacob Silbermann, undergraduate student
[March 2021]

ASG Gallery and Auction Week
Ethan Lewis, undergraduate student
[April 2021]

URBANBuild 2021 Exhibit
[April 2021]

STUDENT EVENTS

Collage Night
Tulane Women in Architecture
[November 2020]

Design Symposium: Designers as Visionaries
Architecture Student Government
Erin Besler
Jackie Sumell
Liz Ogbu
[March 2021]

Wellness Week
Architecture Student Government
AIAS Tulane
Alpha Rho Chi
NOMA Tulane
TuSA Graduate Student Government
[April 2021]

Gallery + Auction
Architecture Student Government
[April 2021]

+ Lecture Series

LECTURES

Human Inhabitation & Equity: Right to the City and Neoliberal Urbanism in the Philippines
Edson G. Cabalfin, Ph.D.
Director of the Social Innovation and Social Entrepreneurship Program, Professor of Practice in Design Thinking, Tulane School of Architecture
[October 2020]

Climate Core: Towards a Common Climate Change Curriculum in the Built Environment
Jesse M. Keenan, Ph.D.
Associate Professor of Real Estate, Tulane School of Architecture
[September 2020]

Graduate Research Symposium
Iñaki Alday, Scott Bernhard, Margarita Jover, Benjamin J. Smith, and Kentaro Tsubaki
[December 2020]

Human Inhabitation & Politics: Super Powers of Scale
Andrés Jaque
Founder, Office for Political Innovation Associate Professor of Professional Practice at Columbia University Graduate School of Architecture, Planning and Preservation
[February 2021]

Human Inhabitation & Development: Migration to Amenity Communities and Development Challenges
Daniela Rivero-Bryant
Lecturer, Master of Sustainable Real Estate Development Program, Tulane School of Architecture
[February 2021]

"I'll teach you differences"
Stanley T. Allen
Professor, Princeton University, Pincipal, Stan Allen Architects
[February 2021]

Human Inhabitation & Health: Embodied Environments
Sara Jensen Carr
Assistant Professor, Northeastern University College of Arts, Media and Design
[March 2021]

Human Inhabitation and Aging: Living Collectively
Mónica Rivera
Partner, Emiliano López Mónica Rivera Arquitectos,
Professor of Practice and Chair of Graduate Architecture in the College of Architecture and Graduate School of Architecture & Urban Design in the Sam Fox of Design & Visual Arts at Washington University in St. Louis
[March 2021]

The ReView

Human Inhabitation & the Natural Environment: Designing Resilient Landscapes
Kate Orff
Founding Principal of SCAPE Studio, Associate Professor and Director of the Center for Resilient Cities and Landscapes at Columbia University Graduate School of Architecture, Planning and Preservation
[March 2021]

Design Justice: Power + Place
Bryan Lee, Jr.
Founder and Design Principal, Colloqate
[March 2021]

2021 Predoctoral Teaching Fellows Lecture
Andrea Bardón de Tena,
Guillermo Lockhart Milán
[April 2021]

Rafael Moneo and the Search for a Reflexive Canon
Francisco González de Canales
Unit Master, Architectural Association London,
Full Professor, University of Seville, Spain,
Principal, Canales-Lombardero
[April 2021]

A Promethean Increment
Albert Pope
Gus Sessions Wortham Professor of Architecture, Rice University
[April 2021]

+

Lecture Series

FACULTY
& STAFF

The ReView

FACULTY 2022-2023

Iñaki Alday
Richard Koch Chair Professor
in Architecture
Dean

Ammar Eloueini
Professor in Architecture

Judith Kinnard
Harvey-Wadsworth Chair
in Landscape Urbanism
Professor in Architecture

Carol McMichael Reese
Favrot IV Professor in Architecture

Kenneth Schwartz
Michael Sacks Chair in Civic Engagement
and Social Innovation
Professor in Architecture
Director of Phyllis M. Taylor Center for
Social Innovation and Design Thinking

Margarita Jover
Professor in Architecture and Landscape
Architecture
Program Director, Landscape Archicture
and Engineering

Scott Bernhard
Associate Professor in Architecture,
Associate Dean for Academics

Michael Crosby
Associate Professor in Architecture

Brent Fortenberry
Mary Louise Mossy Christovich Associate
Professor in Historic Preservation
Program Director, Historic Preservation

Bruce Goodwin
Associate Professor in Architecture

Jesse Keenan
Favrot II Associate Professor in Real State
Development

Tiffany Lin
Favrot V Associate Professor
in Architecture
Program Director, Design

Graham Owen
Associate Professor in Architecture

Wendy Redfield
Associate Professor in Architecture

Kentaro Tsubaki
Favrot I Associate Professor in
Architecture

Fallon Samuels Aidoo
Assistant Professor in Real Estate
Development and Historic Preservation

Rubén García Rubio
Assistant Professor in Architecture
and Urbanism

Hannah Berryhill
Lecturer in Design

Edson Cabalfin
Professor of Practice in Social Innovation
Social Entrepreneurship
Associate Director for Equity, Diversity
and Inclusion
Program Director, SISE

Richard Campanella
Jean and Saul A. Mintz Senior Professor
of Practice
Associate Dean for Research

Bo Choi
Lecturer in Design

John Huppi
Lecturer in Real Estate Development
Associate Program Director, Real Estate
Development

Irene Keil
Senior Professor of Practice

Byron Mouton
Michael G. Lacey Senior Professor
of Practice in Architecture
Director of URBANbuild

Casius Pealer
W. Henry Shane Professor of Practice
in Real Estate Development
Associate Dean for Development
Program director, Real Estate

Daniela Rivero-Bryant
Lecturer in Real Estate Development

Cordula Roser Gray
Senior Professor of Practice
in Architecture

Jill Stoll
Lecturer in Design

Emilie Taylor-Welty
Favrot III Professor of Practice
in Architecture
Program director, Architecture

Sonsoles Vela Navarro
Lecturer in Architecture
Associate Program Director, Architecture

Ann Yoachim
Professor of Practice
Director of the Albert & Tina Small Center
for Collaborative Design

The ReView

Omar Ali
Tulane Architecture & Urbanism Fellow

Nimet Anwar
Visiting Assistant Professor

Jane Ashburn
Research Assistant Professor in Historic
Preservation

Andrea Bardón de Tena
Research Assistant Professor in
Architecture

Will Bradshaw
Visiting Associate Professor in Real Estate
Development

Liz Camuti
Visiting Assistant Professor in Landscape
Architecture

Charles Jones
Visiting Assistant Professor
in Architecture

Emmanuel Osorno
Tulane Architecture & Social Innovation
Fellow

John Park
Visiting Assistant Professor in Real Estate
Development

Megan Saas
Visiting Assistant Professor in Design

+

STAFF

Alexandria Andara
Program Manager, Faculty Employment

José Cotto
Collaborative Design Project Manager,
Albert & Tina Small Center for
Collaborative Design

Christy Crosby
Assistant Dean for Administration
and Operations

Michael J. Cusanza
Assistant Director of Admissions

Andrea Elnems
Director of Finance and Budget

Naomi King Englar
Communications and Marketing Manager

Natalia Fuentes
Program Manager, Academics

Victor Garcia
Technology Manager

Victoria Heffron
Budget & Admininistrative Coordinator II

Sean Huff
Executive Administrative Assistant

Nick Jenisch
Project Manager, Albert & Tina Small
Center for Collaborative Design

Kristen Jones
Assistant Director, Student Affairs

Kyja Jewelweed
Administrative Program Coordinator

Argelle Keller
Administrative Program Coordinator

Nick LiCausi
Director of Fabrication

Hailey Mathieu
Administrative Program Coordinator

Keyoka Nelson
Program Manager, Office and Student
Employment

Emily Parsons
Assistant Dean for Academics and Advising

Catherine Restrepo
Visual Design Coordinator

Jazmine Smith
Web Developer II

The ReView

EMERITY

C. Errol Barron
Emeritus Professor of Architecture

Geoffrey Baker
Emeritus Professor

Eugene D. Cizek
FAIA, Emeritus Professor of Architecture

Karen Kingsley
Emerita Professor

John P.Klingman
Emeritus Professor of Architecture

Richard Powell
Emeritus Professor

John Howell Stubbs
Emeritus Sr. Professor of Practice

Ellen Weiss
Emerita Professor

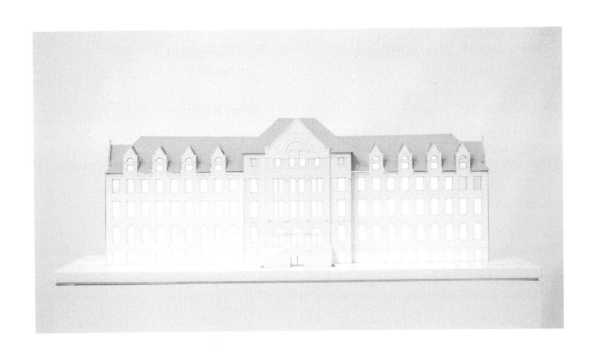

The Review
How & What for

Published by
Actar Publishers, New York, Barcelona
www.actar.com

Edited by
Andrea Bardon de Tena

Publication Assistants
**Gabe Darley, Chelsea Kilgore,
Giuliana Vaccarino Gearty**

Graphic Design
Tulane School of Architecture

Copy editing and proofreading
Alexia Narun

Printing and binding
Arlequin, SL

Distribution
Actar D, Inc. New York, Barcelona.

New York
440 Park Avenue South, 17th Floor
New York, NY 10016, USA
T +1 2129662207
salesnewyork@actar-d.com

Barcelona
Roca i Batlle 2-4
08023 Barcelona, Spain
T +34 933 282 183
eurosales@actar-d.com

Indexing
ISBN: 978-1-63840-070-7
Library of Congress Control Number: 2022946039

Publication date: November 2022

The Review: "How and what for" presents the Tulane
School of Architecture's pedagogical project by
showcasing the work of both students and faculty
over the past few years. The publication is organized
into two main blocks, "how" and "what for". The first
section, "how", offers theoretical course summaries
and a curriculum overview. This contextualizes
TuSA's sequence of studies and its exceptional
pedagogical methodologies. On the other hand, "what
for" situates TuSA's academic work within the social,
economic, and environmental reality architects face
nowadays — highlighting innovative, sometimes
local, projects from faculty and students.

Tulane
School of
Architecture

ACTAR